Marcy's Story

By
TOMMYE W. HAYDEN

Tommye Hayden

Copyright © 2023 by Tommye W. Hayden
All right reserved

No part of this book may be reproduced, or stored in retrieval system, or transmitted in any form of by any means, electronics, mechanical, photocopying, recording, or otherwise, without express written permission of the author.

Cover design by: US BOOK PRESS Printed in the United States of America

Dedication

This book is lovingly dedicated to the Lord, and to those in the medical profession who also serve our Father, and mankind.

Dr. Martin R. White, M.D.

Dr. Ira Emil Carroll, M.D

Dr. M. Vestal Caperton, M. D.

CONTENTS

Discovering God's Will
CHAPTER ONE 1

Total Dependence Upon God
CHAPTER TWO 7

Journey of Faith...the Anointing
CHAPTER THREE 10

The Miracle
CHAPTER FOUR 17

God's Presence
CHAPTER FIVE 20

The Wilderness
CHAPTER SIX 23

Overcoming—Inoperable
CHAPTER SEVEN 36

The Battlefield
CHAPTER EIGHT 50

Frustrated...Yet Standing Firm
CHAPTER NINE 68

Fear Not, God is Able
CHAPTER TEN 81

Brain Lesions... Strong Faith
CHAPTER ELEVEN 92

Hospice
CHAPTER TWELVE 107

The Car Accident...What Next?
CHAPTER THIRTEEN 115

The Move
CHAPTER FOURTEEN 128

Separated
CHAPTER FIFTEEN 131

The Nursing Home
CHAPTER SIXTEEN..144

The Fall
CHAPTER SEVENTEEN 150

Reaching the Goal
CHAPTER EIGHTEEN 166

Great Expectations
CHAPTER NINETEEN 181

Free at Last... The Journey
CHAPTER TWENTY 184

Acknowledgements

My thanks to the many magnificent prayer warriors at First Baptist Church, Conroe, Texas, and Marshall Ford Baptist Church, Austin, Texas, who daily remembered Marcy's needs in prayer throughout her illness. Also to the many friends and relatives who lifted Marcy in prayer before the throne of God.

My thanks to my beloved husband, Brian, who lovingly allowed me to care for Marcy, as we as a family, with God's help, journeyed through their storms.

My thanks to my son, Wallace, who continually helped me because of my inefficient computer skills.

DISCOVERING GOD'S WILL

CHAPTER ONE

Where do I begin? So much has happened, the logical place of course, at the beginning. It is November 1988.

I had been grocery shopping and decided to make a quick stop by my daughter Marcy's house. She is my one child who took up my habit of drinking coffee, and since it was a cold, damp, raw day, coffee with her was just what I needed.

Marcy was a tall vivacious blue-eyed, brown-haired beauty, always with a ready smile, and a happy laugh... yes, coffee and laughter...That would be good.

While sitting at the kitchen table, I noticed a lump on her upper left arm.

"Marcy, what's that lump on your arm?"

"Mother, I have been meaning to show it to you. I found it a few days ago."

"Honey, you need to have it checked. Do you remember injuring it in any way?"

Glancing down at her arm she answered, "No, Mother, it just appeared."

I walked to the phone and called the clinic where I had worked summers a few years ago. Marcia, Dr. Caperton's nurse, said to send her over and they would work her in. Dr. Caperton ordered an x-ray, and after looking at it, he sent her on to the hospital for a MRI. Diagnosis: probable cancer. We discussed it and he felt we should move quickly.

That evening, I called her brother, Wallace, and explained what had been happening. "They are reasonably certain that it's malignant, and they are talking eventually doing surgery. What do you think, son?"

I could hear the shock in his voice as he answered. I had done a rotten job of breaking the news to him about the probability of his big sister having cancer.

After thinking a minute, he answered, "Mother, we live next to one of the best cancer centers in the world. I think that she needs to go to Houston for a consultation appointment."

That evening, after a family conference, we all agreed. The next morning, I called my husband Brian's doctor, Dr. Martin R. White, and asked him what we should do?

He wanted to see her MRI. Brian and I went to the hospital, picked up the MRI and drove to Houston. Dr. White and some colleagues looked at it, and he recommended that we take her to see Dr. Richard Kearns, an orthopedic surgeon who specialized in soft tissue tumors.

The next afternoon, Marcy and I went for a consultation appointment, and we immediately liked Dr. Kearns. He wanted a needle biopsy to determine for sure whether the lump was malignant, and also to see with what type of cancer we were dealing.

On the day of the biopsy, Brian and I drove Marcy to Methodist Hospital in Houston, Texas. In the car, she was apprehensive. In fact, we all were.

"Mother, do you think it's malignant?"

"Honey, I don't know. Surely not, Brian is just now getting well and hopefully, we have had enough sickness for a while... We've had our share."

Brian, my husband, had a rare blood disorder called TTP, and during the past four years, we had been in Methodist Hospital half of that time. We had literally taken up residence in the hospital.

Smiling, I answered, "I have had enough of hospitals to last me a lifetime. Let's not worry until we have to. Whatever happens, remember Honey, in hospital terminology, God is the responsible party for your life, and He has a plan for you. We will leave it to Him."

As I reassured her, I was thinking *please God, please let them be wrong...don't let it be malignant.*

We arrived at the hospital and checked in at day-surgery. A short time later, they took Marcy to surgery. I had brought Dr. Charles Stanley's book HANDLE WITH PRAYER, to read while we waited. I needed to re-adjust my anchor in God so it would hold whatever the outcome. A short time later, Dr. Kearns came to talk to us.

"Everything went well! We have sent the tissue sample to M. D. Anderson Hospital, and we should hear within a week to ten days. Meanwhile, she can go back to work. I'll call when I get the test results."

The next few days seemed like an eternity. Every time the phone rang, I jumped a foot, and my heart pounded in my chest. The thought of Marcy having cancer was overwhelming. She was entirely too young... *Heavenly Father, please, not cancer!* Each day seemed unending.

Marcy's Story

Finally, a week later, Marcy called from her office in Houston. "Mother, Dr. Kearns called. My test results are in. He wants me to come over on my lunch hour to talk to him."

"What time is your lunch hour?"
"It's from one to two, Mother. You don't have to come. The freeway's a zoo at this time of day...I'll be O.K."
"I'm coming, Honey. I'll meet you there."

We both arrived at Dr. Kearns' office at the same time, and we were taken immediately to his office. A short time later, he came in. Looking at him, I knew what he was going to say. The long grueling days and sleepless nights without end had passed... the dreaded moment had arrived.

"Marcy, there's no easy way to say this, so I'll just come right out with it. You have cancer. It is called alveolar soft part sarcoma. It is a very rare deadly form of cancer generally found in the leg. I don't know why the tumor is in your arm, but the treatment will be the same." Shaking his head, he continued, "I'm so sorry!"

For a moment, we were too stunned to speak...we felt trapped in a sense of hopeless despair. There was both shock and terror in our hearts as we both began to cry softly. I could think of nothing to say...no words of comfort, only my tears to add to hers. I felt as though the world was standing still, and my brain had ceased to function. This simply could not be happening. Not cancer! Not Marcy! Why was this happening?

After a few minutes, I was able to speak. "What comes next? What's the plan?"

He sighed and answered. "Marcy, first you will need chemotherapy. We need to shrink the tumor. After chemo, we will do radiotherapy. When your tumor has shrunk from walnut size to pea size, I will operate. How does that sound?"

After a moment, it all began to sink in. Marcy smiled, "I guess we leave it up to you, Dr. Kearns. You know best. Whatever you say. However, I have to tell you, this was not the answer for which we have been hoping and praying."

Dr. Kearns smiled a gentle understanding smile as he nodded his head. "I understand, Marcy. I would like for you to see an oncologist at the Medical Clinic of Houston. She will handle your chemotherapy. I will call her and make an appointment for you. Do you have any questions?"

Sadly, Marcy shook her head. "NO, not at the moment! I will probably think of a million when I get back to my office."

"Marcy, if you think of something, call me. In fact, call me anytime you feel you need to."

For a mother, being told that your daughter has cancer is overwhelming. I turned and gave Marcy a big hug. "Honey, why don't you take the afternoon off? This has been quite a shock."

"I really can't, Mother. This is my third week on a new job, and I simply can't ask for more time especially after taking the day off for the biopsy."

"O.K., Honey, you go on. I will make your financial arrangements. You barely have time to get back. I'll come down tonight, and we will talk when you get home from work. "

As Marcy stood to leave, Dr. Kearns gave her a hug. "Marcy, we are going to make the best possible fight. I will call you about your appointment with the oncologist. We want to start your treatments as soon as possible."

As Marcy left, my thoughts were jumbled with questions.

Marcy's Story

Turning, I said, "Dr. Kearns, you said her cancer was very rare and deadly. Would you please tell me about it? What is her prognosis?" Sighing, he answered, "Bad! They did a case study a few years ago on alveolar soft tissue sarcoma, and out of one hundred cases surveyed, they treated half with chemotherapy and radiation, and they treated the other half with chemotherapy, radiation, and amputation. They had all died in about the same time frame. As far as amputation is concerned, I don't feel it is an option. The tumors are usually fast growing, and it's difficult to shrink them. We will use two of our biggest chemotherapy drugs. If the chemo doesn't do the job we will have to rely on radiation. Any other questions?"

"No," I answered, "I wish we had met under different circumstances, but with God's help, we will make our fight. Marcy is a tremendous Christian, and she is firmly anchored in God. We will ask Him to guide your decisions you will be making for her. Thank you for everything. I guess we will be seeing you soon."

Two days later, we met with the oncologist, and she explained the treatment. There was a possibility Marcy might not survive the chemotherapy. One of the possible side effects of one of the drugs was heart failure. We would not dwell on this. We would make her fight one day at a time. No heart failure allowed!

Three days later, we returned to Houston for a Hickman catheter to be inserted into her subclavian artery...they would access it each for her chemotherapy. Her chemotherapy would begin in one week. She would receive chemotherapy for three days, and then remain in the hospital for an additional two days for observation to make certain her heart and kidneys were functioning properly.

The past few days had seemed as if they were happening to someone else. I had difficulty concentrating on anything. We went through the motions of living our lives daily. I found myself hoping that the phone would ring, and they would tell us it was all a big mistake. Surely, this could not be happening. Not cancer! But it was!

Total Dependence Upon God

CHAPTER TWO

It was time for her first chemotherapy. While staying with her in the hospital, in the middle of the night, the tidal wave hit. Marcy had cancer...a cancer so deadly that the patient usually died within six months to a year! I began to pray.

"Heavenly Father, how can this be happening? I have been caring for Brian for nearly four years, and now this! What's going on?" I was angry, frustrated!

"In everything give thanks for this is the will of Christ Jesus concerning you.
1 Thessalonians 5:18

The Holy Spirit placed this scripture in my mind. Thank Him for her cancer? I can't! Yet, I knew that I had to do this. Through my tears I prayed, I placed Marcy into God's loving hands; the outcome was up to Him. Five minutes later, I found myself pleading with God to take me instead. My children were grown and established, Marcy had a ten-year old daughter, Kristine. What would happen to her? My next thought was *"Lord, I can't stand this...it's too much. First, Brian, now Marcy... too much!"* I knew as I sat there pondering the situation, that I would need a mindset of trust in the person of Christ. Even though I did not understand why this was happening, I would trust Christ to see us through it all. Again, as I sat there, scriptures flooded through my mind.

"There remains then a rest for the people of God; for anyone that enters God's rest also rests from his own work, just as God did from His.

Marcy's Story

"Let us therefore, make every effort to enter that rest, so that no one will fall by following the example of unbelief."
Hebrews 4:9-11

"Let us therefore the throne of grace with confidence so that we may receive mercy grace to help us in our time of need."
Hebrews 4:16 (NIV)

By faith, I would turn the situation over to God for His solution, and I would trust Him for her healing. I would faith rest it... otherwise it would be unbearable. As a family, we would have to enter God's rest.

I began praying. *"Lord, she is your child... Your way not mine... I give her to You... Your will be done."* I felt an immediate peace... this time I would hold on, no matter what.

When we faith-rest a situation, we must seek God's peace.

If we become like leaves being blown in the wind, we cannot glorify God.

"God is our refuge and strength, ever present help in trouble. Therefore, we will not fear."
Psalm 42:1-2a

I sat there thinking...without God how could we handle this? He would truly have to be our refuge as we journeyed through these next months.

Marcy was becoming restless.

"Mother, I'm really feeling sick. Can you call the nurse for me?"

I pushed the button for the nurse and explained that Marcy was nauseated. She came in a few minutes later with a syringe of decadron, and she slowly injected it into Marcy's catheter.

A few minutes later, the nausea passed and Marcy went back to sleep. The next morning, she began drinking gallons of water. The nurses explained to us that water would help flush the chemo from her body, and it would help her to not become nauseous. She finished her chemo without any big nausea problems. We discovered that if she forced liquids and ate, regardless of how she was feeling, the nausea was bearable. God was good!

Marcy resigned from her job. The doctors wanted her to get plenty of rest between her chemotherapy treatments. This would also benefit her heart.

I thanked God for the spiritual growth I had been experiencing during Brian's illness. For months, he had not been expected to live, and as I looked back through my prayer journal, I saw God's continual presence, moment by moment, as He had answered prayers on Brian's behalf. I began to realize that Brian's illness had been my training ground for Marcy's cancer.

Journey of Faith...the Anointing

CHAPTER THREE

One morning as I was fasting and praying about Marcy, I knew in my heart things were not looking good. Each month after her chemotherapy, the tumor would shrink, but because the tumor was so fast growing, by the end of the month it would be back to its original size. She wasn't making any headway at all.

During my quiet time, I asked the Holy Spirit for some words of assurance... something about living. As I began reading my Bible, the following scripture spoke to my heart, and I felt I had God's answer.

"Deal bountifully with thy servant, that I may live keep your word."

Psalm 119: 7

I felt God had answered my prayer. Marcy was going to live. I typed this scripture on a card with some others concerning fear. These scriptures would be a part of her "survival kit," a part of her healing. She would use these promises, always remembering that whenever we take a step-in faith to achieve something, everything in heaven is behind us to help us accomplish it. These scriptures would be her mainstays when Satan caused doubts to enter her mind saying that she was going to die.

I drove down to her house. She was in the kitchen having coffee.

"Hi Honey! How are you feeling this morning?" I could see that she had been crying.

"What's wrong?"

"I'm OK, Mother. My head is sensitive and sore, and my hair is just downright painful every morning when I wash it. It's getting so thin. Would you cut it short for me? Maybe it won't look so bad. I don't want to have to start wearing a wig to church on Sundays yet.

Every time I put my wig on, I feel like it's strangling me."

I smiled, and answered, "Sure, come on."

We walked down the hall to the bathroom and she sat down on the stool. I picked up the scissors and began cutting. I looked into the mirror to see how I was doing, and saw that she was crying. I began to cry too. I bent over and put my arms around her, hugging her, and we cried together. Every time we attempted to talk; we both would cry harder.

While holding her, in my mind, I began to pray. *"Heavenly Father, we can't do this without your help. I love her so much. You know how she helped me raise her brother and sister while I worked three jobs trying to support us the eight years, I was a single parent. She's worked so hard...she doesn't deserve this. Please, God, don't take my child... please heal her, please! Let her have a chance to enjoy life. She's earned it! Give her the time to finish raising Kristine, in Jesus' name I pray, Amen."*

After a time, I straightened and raised my head. As I looked at her with anguished eyes, with tears streaming down my face, I saw her smiling through her tears.

"Mother, this is silly. What are we crying about? A lot of people shave their heads. At least I have some hair left. It will grow back. Remember when we were getting my wig at M. D. Anderson Hospital, the volunteer said brown headed people often came back auburn colored. You've always said you wished you had red hair...well, get ready...I'm going to be a gorgeous redhead one of these days. Picture that!"

As always, she had turned our tears to laughter.

A short time later, I remembered the reason I had come to see her.

"Hey, good news! This morning, in my quiet time, God gave me the best scripture. I've typed it on a card for you with some others. I want you to pray through them every morning during your quiet time.

Everything's going to be fine. Daily, I want you to visualize your body healthy and whole. Thank God that He's healing you, and with His help, you are going to be healed. From this minute on, doubt is out!"

I handed her the card, and she began to read.

> *"Deal bountifully with me, that I may live and keep your word."*
> *Psalms 119: 7*

> *"When I am afraid, I will trust in you."*
> *Psalms 56:3 (NIV)*

> *"You may ask me for anything in my name, and I will do it."*
> *John 14:14 (NIV)*

> *"If you believe, you will receive whatever you ask for in prayer."*
> *Matthew 21:22 (NIV)*

> *"...Ask and you shall receive that your joy may be full."*
> *John 16:24*

Marcy's Story

"Therefore, I tell you, whatever you ask for in prayer, believe that you have received it, and it will be yours."
Mark 11:24 (NIV)

"Be strong and courageous! Do not tremble or be dismayed, for the Lord your God is with you wherever you go."
Joshua 1:9

"Do not be afraid or discouraged...for the battle is not yours, but God's." *11 Chronicles 20:15b, c (NIV)*

"You will not have to fight this battle. Take up your positions; stand firm and see the deliverance the Lord will give you."
11 Chronicles 20:17a, b (NIV)

She finished reading. "Mother, these are great...just what I need."

"Marcy, from now on, whenever fear strikes, I want you to tap into the presence of God, direct your gaze on Him instantly, and tell Him you are depending on Him for your healing. Then get your card and pray through these scriptures knowing and believing that God is handling your situation."

"Honey, there is one other thing. There is a passage in the New Testament concerning healing. It gives specific instructions on what we are to do. I would like to call your Uncle Everett, and ask him to come and read James 5:13-16, anoint you with oil, and pray for God to heal you. How about it?"

"Mother, I know God's promises are for us to claim in faith. I have everything to gain, I'm ready...let's call!"

I walked over to the phone and called my brother-in-law, Dr. Everett Reneer, and asked when he could come over and anoint her. We set a time for the following morning at ten.

Marcy's Story

"Marcy, I need to get home. If you need anything call me. I'll pick you up in the morning so you won't have to drive."

Morning came. It was bright and beautiful. A gentle rain had fallen during the night. Everything was fresh and clean as only God could make it...a perfect day for her anointing. I drove down to get Marcy, and as usual, she was ready and waiting.

Smiling, I said, "Good morning, Honey. How was your night?"

"Much better, Mother. My head has really been painful. Cutting my hair was the pits, but it was the best thing we could have done. Last night, it didn't pain me every time I turned over.

I don't know why I didn't ask you to cut it sooner. How are you, Mother?"

"I'm great! I know we are doing what God would have us to do... I'm excited."

As we turned into the driveway, we discovered that Everett and my sister, Marcine, were already there.

I had made a fresh pot of coffee before I left. We hugged our hellos! Turning to Everett, I asked, "Are you ready?"

Everett smiled and answered, "Why don't we all sit down at the table and have coffee. I want to talk to all of you for a few minutes." Everett had taught theology and pastoral care in two of our Southern Baptist seminaries before he and my sister, Marcine, moved to Conroe, Texas, to begin a Christian counseling center. We had our very own elder and pastor teacher in the family.

Sis and I poured the coffee. As we sat down Everett explained that it was not always God's will that every person be healed. Certainly, we should follow God's instructions in anointing

Marcy with oil and praying for her, but the outcome was totally in God's hands. We all agreed that this was scriptural. He suggested we go into the living room. We placed a chair in the center of the room, and Marcy sat down in it. We made a circle around her, and placed our hands on her as Everett read:

> *"Is any one of you in trouble? He should pray. Is anyone happy? Let him sing songs of praise. Is any one of you sick? He should call the elders of the church to pray over him anoint him with oil in the name of the Lord. And the prayer offered in faith will make the sick person well; the Lord will raise him up. If he has sinned, he will be forgiven. Therefore, confess your sins to each other and pray for each other that you may be healed. The prayer of a righteous man is powerful and effective."*
>
> *James 5:13-16 (NIV)*

After reading the scriptures, Everett dipped his finger into the bowl of olive oil and anointed her on the forehead. He suggested we close with prayer. After praying, we walked slowly to the kitchen. We did not speak. We had strongly felt the presence of the Holy Spirit, and the moment was too precious for words. After a few minutes, I thanked them for coming, and they left for their counseling center.

"Marcy, why don't you stay and have lunch with us? I made tuna salad earlier this morning. I'll take you home in time for your nap. I know you have to get your rest."

"That sounds great. I can't remember when I last had tuna."
After lunch, I drove her home. As we turned into the driveway, I turned and smiled. "Honey, as we prayed, I felt God's presence and His peace. I feel that God is going to honor our prayer for your healing. I'm so sorry you've had to do battle for your life, and go through what you've gone through, but with God's help you are going to make it."

Marcy's Story

"Remember, from now on, be positive, think positive... you are healed! We will turn your situation over to God, and we will ask Him to guide all of the choices your physicians will be making on your behalf. The outcome will be totally in His Hands. We will faith rest your cancer. Agreed?"

"Agreed, Mother. Mother, you've always been there for us. You've always pointed us toward God with your life style. Words are inadequate to tell you how I feel, but I want you to know that I love you. I want to thank you for all you do, and for all that you have done. I don't want you to worry. I'm really fine with this."

As I drove toward our house, I thought back through the years, after their dad and I were divorced, how truly blessed I had been with my three children. At the time of the divorce, Marcy, age twelve, Marilyn, age nine, and Wallace, age seven... all three had been so trustworthy. They each had taken responsibility for themselves and for each other.
I was in my first year of college at the University of Texas in El Paso working towards a Bachelor's degree in music education when their dad had left. I did not have the money to hire someone to stay with Wallace, and being in the second grade, he had to spend an hour alone every afternoon until his two sisters arrived home from school. Throughout college, as I had struggled to carry twenty-two to twenty-three semester hours in order to graduate in three and one-half years instead of the usual five years, they had given me moral and physical support in every way. I took classes in the morning, and worked in the music department afternoons for my tuition, books and a small salary.

The girls had done the housework and cooking, and Wallace had done the yard work. We had truly been blessed. God had helped us make every important decision, and I knew for certain in my heart that He would be there for us now. He had promised in His Word, *"I will never leave you or forsake you,"* and I knew it to be true.

The Miracle

CHAPTER FOUR

Marcy's chemotherapy treatment was complete. Now it was radiation time. The tumor had withstood everything, and had not shrunk. She would have radiation for four days a week for three weeks, and after her arm healed Dr. Kearns would do her surgery. After the first week, they changed her radiation to five days a week, and had decided to increase her treatment time from three weeks to six weeks. The doctor explained that alveolar sarcoma tumors were known to be rapid growing and deadly, and he did not want to take any chances. We explained that we were leaving all the decisions to him. We were praying for God to give him guidance in all the decisions made for her... so, whatever he felt, it was fine with us.

Brian did a large part of the driving as we made our daily trips to Houston for her radiation treatments. While in the waiting room, we met a lot of hurting, suffering people. Children, mothers with small babies, young, old...all with one thing in common...all had cancer. We experienced a new awareness of how precious, indeed, life was, and we would attempt to live each day *"as unto the Lord."* As we waited for her in the waiting room, we had many opportunities to share what God was doing in Marcy's life.

Her radiation was complete, and we began the waiting period for surgery. Again, the tumor had stayed the same, and the outcome did not look good. On Friday, when Dr. Kearns did his pre-op physical, he explained that, because of the size of her tumor, he would have to do reconstructive surgery at a later date.

Marcy's Story

Her arm would be there for cosmetic purposes only, and because he would have to remove a large part of her upper arm it would not have much function. She would probably have to wear it in a sling. Again, we explained that from the beginning we had asked God to guide all the choices he would make on her behalf, so we were comfortable with any decision he would make. We would leave everything to him and to our heavenly Father. We were asking God to be in control over his hands as he operated. He smiled and said, "I need all the help I can get."

As we were leaving, he hugged Marcy and said, "I'm going to do my best."

Sunday came, and we all went to Sunday school and church. Marcy and I had agreed that we would ask our Sunday school departments to join us in prayer, asking God to shrink her tumor so her arm would not be useless.

Monday came, and Marcy went to surgery. As her husband, Gene, and I sat in the waiting room, God gave me the most wonderful peace. Prayerfully, I placed Marcy in His hands, and I felt His wonderful presence during the three hours we waited. Even though the time seemed an eternity, I knew all was well.

After surgery, Dr. Kearns came to talk to us. He was beaming as he said, "The tumor had shrunk. It was self-contained, and it had not moved into the lymph nodes. Her arm will have full function with physical therapy, and reconstructive surgery will not be necessary. How's that for a good report?"

I smiled and answered, "Thank you, God is good! We asked our church family yesterday to pray for God to shrink the tumor, and since it had not shrunk on Friday, and it was pea size this morning...I believe God gave us our first miracle. Thank you again... we appreciate you."

Marcy's Story

Our family, church family, and friends had all prayerfully supported us during the months before and after Marcy's surgery. They provided food, and had even taken over Christmas while we were busy with her treatments. Without Christ, without the presence of the Holy Spirit as our constant companion, dealing with her cancer would have been unthinkable and unbearable.

God answered prayer, and He gave us our miracle! I discovered an old truth anew... God's will for our lives will never lead us through a valley where the grace of God and His mercy is not adequate for the trial. Once again, we had realized that when you have a problem that does not have an earthly solution, by faith, give it to God...rest in Him! He alone is able to deliver you.

God's Presence

CHAPTER FIVE

Marcy's recovery was incredible. Each week she went for a dressing change, and once a month for a chest x-ray. Dr. Kearns was sure she was not going to have any problems with her lungs, but he was going to take precautions to make sure all was well. Two months after her surgery, he allowed her to go back to work. She would have monthly x-rays. He explained that he wanted to keep a careful watch during the first year.

She began searching for a job. They were a two-income family, so her working was a necessity. A short time later, she went for an interview with a credit bureau in Greenspoint. We were hoping she could find a teacher's aide job in Conroe, and not have to commute any more.

This however, was not God's plan for her. She was going to be a data entry clerk.

She began her new job. The commute was much better than driving to down town Houston. She immediately made new friends, and after a short time, suggested they have a Bible Study one day each week during their lunch hour.

Her hair had grown back. It had come in snow white and curly. It was beautiful. Her hair had always been fine, but now it had a marvelous texture. She wanted to color it, but Gene didn't want her to so she submitted and let it stay white.

Time passed swiftly, and it was time for her six months checkup. I drove down and we went together. She was feeling

Marcy's Story

wonderful, so we were not concerned. I had not seen Dr. Kearns since the day of her surgery. He examined her arm, and sent her for an x-ray. A short time later, he went over and read the x-ray.

He was smiling as he entered the room. "Everything looks good. You won't need to come back until your anniversary date in December. How is that for good news?"

Marcy answered, "It sounds wonderful to me. I will miss our monthly visits; however, it will be a good miss. We will see you in December. Thanks again for everything, you're the best."

As we drove back to her office, I was thanking God for her good news.

"Honey, as long as I'm in Greenspoint Mall, I think I will do some shopping. Do you need anything?"

"No, Mother, I'm OK! Thanks for coming down to go with me. It wasn't necessary, but I'm glad you came. You're the nicest!"

I shopped for a couple of hours, and didn't find any 'purple.' 'Purple,' is when you need something specific, and you've asked God for it at a certain price, and you go into the store, and there it is waiting for you. You know God has answered your prayers, so it's yours. I talk to my Heavenly Father about all things. After all, we have a promise that *"He will supply all our needs"*, so why not? Of course, I want it to be in keeping with His will for me...He always knows what's best for me. Sometimes, I discover when I can't find something I think I can't survive without, a couple of months later I'm grateful I didn't find it, because it wasn't really what I needed in the first place. I don't just pray about the big things; I pray about everything. It keeps me from making a lot of mistakes.

As I drove home, I was thanking God that all was well. Both Marcy and Brian were recovered...life was truly good.

Marcy's Story

The days and months flew past. It was time for Marcy's first year check-up. Once again, I drove down and picked her up in Greenspoint, and we drove on to Dr. Kearn's office.

He checked the tumor site carefully, and sent her for an x-ray. After the x-ray we returned to his office for the results. As we waited in the treatment room, we were discussing how well she was feeling, and how God had answered prayer on her behalf.

"Mother, during the dark moments when I first discovered I had cancer, I always felt it was going to be O.K. I felt God's continual presence, and I know that He had a purpose in allowing my cancer. A number of people have told me that as our church prayed for my healing, they felt it had brought our church family closer together. As I journeyed through the dark moments, I was always moving toward the 'Light,' toward Jesus… it was in life or death, He was with me. I praise Him for all He has done."

Dr. Kearns walked in beaming. "Marcy, everything's great… couldn't be better. There was an eighty percent chance your tumor would grow back during your first year. I didn't tell you because I didn't want you to worry until it became necessary. All is well! You passed with flying colors.

As we were leaving, I turned to thank him. "We are so grateful for all you have done. We appreciate you. With God's help, you have restored Marcy back to good health."

Dr. Kearns smiled and pointed towards heaven and said, "More Him than me."

As usual, as we were leaving, he gave Marcy a big hug. "I'll see you in June."

Marcy's Story

The Wilderness

CHAPTER SIX

The years passed quickly. Marcy continued commuting to Greenspoint to her supervisor job. I continually thanked the Lord she was alive. Dr. Kearns checked her tumor site and x-rayed a year. All was well.

Her fifth anniversary was here. She called and made her appointment with Dr. Kearns. We were sure everything was fine so I didn't go. Six months earlier everything had been clear and we were confident this check-up would reveal the same.

After Dr. Kearns read her x-ray, he came to talk to her.

"Marcy, I think we need to do an MRI. I see some cloudy areas on your lungs. I don't think it's anything to worry about, but I want to be sure. I want to schedule an MRI appointment. I'll call you when they have an opening."

"Dr. Kearns, can you call Mother instead? I don't want anyone at work to know that I've had cancer. You never know when you are going to find someone who's afraid that cancer is contagious. I discovered the hard way that sometimes when you mention the word cancer, some people are immediately afraid of you.

"That will be fine."

Marcy called me later that afternoon while on her break from the employee lounge.

"Mother, Dr. Kearns wants to do an MRI. My lungs have some cloudy areas. He feels that everything is fine. This is just a

Marcy's Story

precaution. He will call you the appointment time. I was afraid someone would overhear our conversation if I were at my desk. Do you mind taking his call?

"Of course not, honey! He really thinks that everything's O.K.

"Yes, mother, I'll call you tonight when I get home from work."

The phone rang a short time later. It was Dr. Kearns' office. Her MRI would be the following Friday.

Friday came and Marcy went for her MRI. When we talked, she insisted on my not coming. "Mother, I can do this by myself. It isn't necessary for you to drive to Houston. I will be fine."

She disliked having MRI'S alone. The tunnel was entirely too small. I generally sat at her head and talked with her between the shoots. Her hearing had been severely compromised from the chemotherapy drugs she had taken. One of the possible side effects from one of the drugs was hearing loss, and with the nerve damage she was already experiencing, the two combined had taken her hearing. She wore a hearing aid, and read lips so well people rarely knew she had a hearing problem.

I shared with her that when I had my MRI after I fractured my skull on the refrigerator, while in the tunnel, I quoted every scripture I had ever memorized, and before I knew it, I was being taken out. My Father's word had been my comfort. It would be hers, too.

The MRI was complete and she returned to work. The remainder of the week passed slowly. We were not really worried, she had been given six months to a year to live, five years ago, and we were confident she had been healed. It would be a relief, however, for Dr. Kearns to call and tell us it had been a false alarm.

He called Marcy's office the following Wednesday.

"Marcy, I need to see you. When can you come in?"

Surprised, she answered, "I can run over on my lunch hour.

Will that be O.K. with you?"
"Yes, come on! We need to talk."
A little later Marcy called. "Mother, Dr. Kearns called. I'm going over on my lunch hour to talk to him. You don't need to come—there's not enough time for you to get here anyway. Just pray it's nothing serious. I'll call you this afternoon when I'm on my break."

"Marcy, honey, I think I should come."

"Mother, there just isn't time. I think if it had been too serious, he would have just come out and told me. You know he's not only my doctor, he's my friend, too. Don't worry, pray. Isn't that what you always say? I'll call soon."

The minute I hung up the phone, I began to have misgivings. I should have insisted they wait for me to come. Fragmented thoughts were rushing around in my head. A million *'what ifs'* were bombarding my mind. I had to seek God's peace.

"Do not be anxious about but in everything, by prayer and petition, with thanksgiving, present your requests to God. And the peace of God, which transcends all understanding, will guard your hearts and your minds in Christ Jesus."
Philippians 4:6-7 (NIV)

I began to pray. "Father, she's already gone through so much, please don't let her be sick again. Let it be something minor. Please, Father, please?"

I had long since discovered that when we have the peace of God reigning in our hearts, with His help, we can face any circumstances that come our way. God assumes the responsibility for providing our peace. God's Spirit sometimes reminds us of a scripture that fits the problem we are experiencing, and this gives us assurance that He's with us...He's in control. The following scripture flashed through my mind.

"God is our refuge strength, an ever-present help in trouble. Therefore, we will not fear..."
Psalm 46:1-2a (NIV)

We are to make our petitions to God... tell him our circumstances, what's troubling us, and ask for His peace.

The truth of the matter, I was afraid. The *"what ifs"* were back. Again, I turned my thoughts to God's word. I would refuse to be anxious. I would trust Him for her situation.

I sat by the phone, willing it to ring. A short time later it rang. I was in such a hurry to answer that I dropped it. I knew it was Marcy before I answered.

There was total silence on the other end.

"Marcy, is this you? What's wrong?" Still nothing...no response.
"Talk to me, honey." I both wanted and dreaded to hear what she had to say. My heart began to pound and my skin grew clammy... I felt so weak I was having difficulty holding the phone to my ear.

"Mother, I..." She began to cry softly. For a moment she said nothing. She finally spoke in a voice empty of hope. "Mother, my diagnosis is sarcoma metastatic to the lung. I have four lesions, two in each lung. One large and one small in my right lung, and two small ones in my left lung."
I sat there stunned with a knot in my chest and a lump in my throat. My eyes began to sting with hot tears. After a few

minutes I was able to speak.

"Marcy, where are you? Are you coming home?"

"No, Mother, I'm here in the employee lounge alone. I'm trying to get my act together so I can go downstairs. I need to get back to work.

Right now, I need to keep busy so I can keep my mind off what's happening. I'm late! I'll be O.K. I'll call you tonight when I get home. I love you! Bye!" She quickly hung up the phone. I knew that she was barely keeping it together. She was incapable of talking more at the moment.

I should have known the news would not be good when Dr. Kearns wanted to see her. I should have insisted they wait for me to come. Instead, she'd had to face this terrible news by herself. We were both still crying as she hung up the phone.

I felt frozen in time. I was weighed down with despair. I couldn't believe what she had told me...not lung cancer, this couldn't be happening - not again... it simply was not fair.

I began to pray. "Father, I can't deal with this. We thought she was healed. Why does she have to go through more suffering...I don't understand."

I know that when our world crashes in around us, we are to turn to our Heavenly Father for comfort. I was angry! I felt violated. More sickness—too much! I knew from working for my doctors during the summer, that once a person was diagnosed with metastatic lung cancer, it was just a matter of time.

The remainder of the day passed slowly. Nothing seemed real. I couldn't seem to concentrate on anything very long. Over and over in my mind the thoughts tumbled, Marcy has lung cancer.

Marcy's Story

Unless God intervenes, she's going to die. I went to the bedroom and closed the door and began to pray.

"Father, I know I have to be strong. Right this moment, I feel like a basket case. I thought Marcy was through with cancer forever. I thought she was healed. I know You tell us in Your Word, in Romans 8:28, "In everything give thanks, for this is the will of Christ Jesus concerning you." I know You engineer our circumstances for our good and Your glory. I know this is Your will for Marcy, Your plan her life, for us as a family.

Help us to be strong. Give us Your peace and Your courage to face this crisis. Please comfort Marcy right now...right this minute. Let her feel Your presence as she is attempting to finish her day at the office. Her anguish must be almost unbearable. Please comfort her as only You can. Father, it seems impossible to thank You for her cancer, but I yield. You tell us, to give thanks—how I, yet, I know I must. You tell us, "All things work together for our good—how can this be good? Good? More cancer? Oh, Father, I know You are with us in the dark moments of our life. I know You have a purpose in allowing the dark moments. I know this is Your training ground for higher service. I know our dark moments are always for our good. I know we learn more in the dark moments than in the light, so please, Father, help us not to be afraid, not to be frustrated, not to rebel against this situation... help us to be able to give thanks. Give us Your peace! I praise You and thank you for Marcy's cancer. She's your child... I give her to You. Strengthen and comfort us as family and with Your help, once again we will make this fight, in Jesus' name I pray, Amen!"

As I left my bedroom, I felt God's peace. I wanted to talk to Dr. Kearns. I needed to know what he was thinking. I placed the call and asked that he return my call as soon as possible. A short time later the phone rang.

"Hello!"

"This is Dr. Kearns. I'm really sorry about Marcy. Her test results were a shock for all of us. I'm very surprised. I had hoped she was through with cancer when it had not spread to the lymph nodes around the tumor site. Her lungs must have been seeded while we were attempting to shrink the tumor before surgery."

I was struggling to hold back my tears. "Dr. Kearns, what are you thinking in regard to her treatment?"

"After I reviewed her MRI results, I spoke with a specialist who does thoracic surgery. There are two courses of treatment. We can do chemotherapy again only, or we can do surgery and chemo combined. The surgical procedure is called thoracotomy. At the moment, I'm not sure which course we should follow. I have asked Dr. Jim Garza to read her MRI, and give us his recommendation. Once again, we will want to begin her treatment as quickly as possible. You will need to be thinking about the situation, too. I took the liberty of making a consultation appointment with him on Friday, at 4:00 p.m. Marcy wanted to take off a little early and not lose a full day. Can you make it?"

"Yes, I'll be there. Dr. Kearns, thank you for everything you are doing. You are a wonderful caring doctor...truly special. I'll call you after we see Dr. Garza."

The remainder of the week, as a family, we did some serious praying. We wanted God's guidance in making the choice.

Dr. Garza had operated on Brian when he had his aneurysm, so we knew him to be one of the Medical Center's finest cardiovascular and thoracic surgeons. He had also done her catheter for her chemo, so we were comfortable with Dr. Kearns' choice of surgeons.

I called Dr. White, explained what had been happening, explained the choices, and asked what he would do? He said he wanted to think about it, and he would call me.

He called me early the next morning. He had spent a large part of the night at his computer looking for possible treatments. He was undecided. He explained if she had the surgery, her recovery would be long and painful. He was not certain surgery would give her that much more time, but regardless of which treatment we pursued, her quality of life would be better with the chemotherapy only. He said it was indeed a tough call to make.

Friday came. I drove to Marcy's office, and we drove on to Dr. Garza's office together.

He came briskly into the treatment room.

"Mrs. King, I have seen your MRI. I would like to listen to your lungs and heart, do a brief physical, and then I'll give you, my recommendation."

He spent the next few minutes examining her carefully.

"You have four lesions—one large tumor, and three small ones. I feel your odds would be better with surgery. The large tumor will require a large incision. You will have a circular cut from under your right breast around to your back. I will remove both tumors in your right lung through this incision. It will be very painful afterwards. During the surgery, I will cut some of the nerves, and this will greatly help the pain factor. It will be at least six months before you feel yourself again. I will do the two small tumors on your left lung with small incisions. I want you to understand it will be extremely painful. This, however, is what I recommend."

Marcy turned quietly to me, smiled, and then to Dr. Garza.
"To be honest, I want to pray about this. I want to know God's plan for me in this. I will let you know my decision soon. Thank you for all the information."

Nodding his head, "I understand," he answered, "I'll be waiting to hear from you."

As we were driving back to her office, she turned. "Mother, what do you really think about all this?"

"Honey, I simply don't know. Let's ask our church family to join us in prayer concerning this decision. I guess chemo only would certainly be the easy way, but we want you to have the best possible chance. I'm going to call Dr. Carroll, and see what he thinks. We'll have to rely on God to help us make this decision. We definitely need to know God's will in this. We'll gather all the information we can, and with God's help, we'll decide. Marcy, ride to Conroe with me. Let's leave your car and I'll drive you to work in the morning. I don't want you to be alone right now.

"Mother, I'm fine...as good as I can be with all that has happened. We will make the choice after the weekend...after our prayer warriors from church join us in asking for God's guidance. Agreed?"

"Agreed!"

As I looked at her, it was apparent how hard she was trying to maintain control of herself. I didn't want to leave her. She sat quietly gathering her thoughts. She looked with unseeing eyes. Turning, she smiled, "Mother, I know from past experience, the more I trust in God, the more I know for certain He never lets us down... He's always constant... with God's help, I can do this."

As I drove to Conroe, I was once again weighed down with despair. I prayed for God to make His will known to us. We truly wanted His choice.

Saturday dawned bright and clear. I hadn't slept much. My

Marcy's Story

mind kept replaying all the things the doctors had explained to us. It was a grim and terrible situation. I had spent the night thinking and praying.

I waited until ten a.m. to call Dr. Carroll... didn't want to wake him. Dr. Carroll had helped to raise my children. I had taught school, done the music in various churches, and had worked summers at his clinic for a number of years. As a single parent I always needed more money. Best of all, however, he was a true friend. One we had relied on. He answered the phone on the third ring.

"This is Dr. Carroll." His voice sounded the same. He had left Conroe six months earlier to retire.

"Good morning! This is Tommye. How are things in Albuquerque?" I could hear the surprise in his voice as he answered.

"We are enjoying it here. I've had to learn to breathe here in the higher altitude—but all things considered, we like it. How are you and Brian?"

"We are fine. I'm calling about Marcy. Her cancer has returned. Her diagnosis, sarcoma, metastatic to the lung. She has four lesions, one large and one small lesion in her right lung, and two small lesions in her left lung. We were referred to Dr. Jim Garza, and he discussed two treatments, a thoracotomy to remove the tumors, and then chemo, or chemotherapy only. We need some help on this decision. What do you think?"

After a time, he spoke. "Tommye, as you know sarcoma is a rare deadly form of cancer. I think she stands a better chance of survival with both surgery and chemo. It will buy her more time. The surgery, however, is extremely painful... requires a big incision...a difficult recovery. She will need a lot of TLC (tender loving care). If she were mine this is what I would do. I'm so sorry about this. I had hoped she was through with cancer."

"Me too! This really took us by surprise. For years, you have helped make our medical choices, so naturally I had to ask you about this. We really miss you... in fact, Conroe misses you." We talked on a few minutes, catching up on our family news.

After we hung up, I felt better. I had confidence that he had helped us in making the right choice. A short time later I called Marcy.

"Hi! I just talked to Dr. Carroll. He and Jane like Albuquerque. I asked about what we should do about you, and he thinks you should have both surgery and chemotherapy. After church tomorrow, after we ask for special prayer, I think we will know what God would have us do where you are concerned... His plan for you. I am so thankful we are rooted and grounded in God. This would be impossible to accept otherwise. Honey, how are you feeling?"

"I'm O. K. Most of the time, I can accept this as God's will for me at this point in time. The rest of the time, I find myself thinking, *why Lord, why me ...why now?* I know Romans 8:28 states, *"And we know that in all things God works for the good of those who have been called according to his purpose."* I know in my heart that this will work for my good, but it's really tough to accept. More pain, more suffering, more surgery, more chemo... at the moment, in all honesty, I'm not looking forward to what lies ahead. I know what you are thinking Mother, we will make it one day at a time... and I know with God's help, we will...but it's still hard. Mother, Gene is in the car. We were leaving to go to the grocery store. I'll call you tomorrow after church. I love you, Mother---don't worry, we'll make it!"

I hung up the phone with a heavy heart. She had been through so much... and now this.

Sunday dawned bright and clear. At Sunday school, when we were requesting prayer for loved ones, and friends in need, I explained what was happening with Marcy. Everyone was surprised, just as we had been. I asked them to pray that God would make His will known concerning her treatment. Carl Kennedy, our department superintendent, asked Paul Gilliam to pray a special prayer for her. As Paul prayed, I felt immediate comfort. We further agreed to pray to ask God to make His will known for Marcy. Now we would await His answer.

The day passed slowly. I had a calmness and peace in my heart. God was at work...all was well. After praying, I felt she was to have both surgery and chemotherapy. I felt God had answered our prayers. I would wait to hear from her. Late that evening, the phone rang.

"Mother, I wanted to call you. Today has been an unusual day. All day, I felt God's comforting presence as I prayed. I have been listening in my heart for God's guidance. I feel I'm to have both surgery and chemo. I'm totally at peace with my decision. What are you thinking?"

"I arrived at that same conclusion... I think we know God's will, so let's get the wheels in motion. I was waiting to hear from you."

"Mother, can you call Dr. Kearns and Dr. Garza in the morning. I really need to go to work. I can't afford to take any more time off until I have to. Set the surgery date as soon as possible. When the arrangements are made, call me, and I will talk to my boss. I'll be waiting to hear from you. Thanks Mother, for always being there when I need you...you're the nicest!"

Monday came, and I called Dr. Garza's office. I explained I

was calling for Marcine King, and that she wanted me to set up a surgery time. They said they would call me back when they could get her on the schedule.

Just before noon, they called. Her surgery would be the following Thursday morning. After surgery she would be in intensive care for at least forty-eight hours. Then she would be placed in a room for about a week, and then home. It would be a month before she could do anything, so we would need to arrange someone to care for her during the day. After she healed in, they would begin her chemotherapy. She would need to take at least six weeks sick leave. We would know more about the chemo after Dr. Garza did the surgery.

I called her and told her the plan. She decided she would work right up to the day before the surgery. I wanted her to take some time off so she would be rested for her surgery.

"Mother, I will have six weeks to rest, and I need to work. I'm fine. Besides, the week would be years long if I didn't stay busy.

I'll call you tonight." We hung up the phone. She was right, the week was going to seem like an eternity.

Overcoming—Inoperable

CHAPTER SEVEN

Thursday came Marcy, Gene and I left for Methodist Hospital at 4:30 a.m. She was to check in by 6 a.m. As we drove down, not much was said. We were each praying for what lay ahead. I felt in my heart that all was going to be well. It would be a relief to have her surgery over.

Her check-in was well organized and uneventful. We stayed with her until they took her to surgery.

"Honey, I feel good about this, Dr. Garza is going to be God's hands on earth this morning as he operates on you. Let's have a quick prayer."

"Heavenly Father, thank you that you are in control of every facet of our lives. We realize that as Your children, nothing comes into our lives unless You allow it. We ask that You guide Dr. Garza's hands the choices he will make on her behalf. We ask that You continue to give us all Your peace as we face this adversity. I give her to You... I praise You that she's Your child. Be with her. Thank you, in Jesus name we pray, Amen."

We gave her a kiss as they took her away, and then we went to the surgery waiting room.

I had brought Dr. Charles Stanley's book, ADVANCING THROUGH ADVERSITY, to read while we waited. I needed to stay focused on God, otherwise I would go straight to panic palace. The waiting room was crowded. Gene and I were not able to get chairs together, so I could read and continue trusting

Marcy's Story

God for the outcome without feeling I had to make conversation with him. As the people around me saw the title of the book, they began asking questions about it. I explained that there was a tape series that accompanied it and it was wonderful. As we shared what was going on in the lives of our loved ones we were waiting for, it gave me an opportunity to share what God had already done for Marcy five years earlier.

The doctors began coming out to talk to the families. Some of the surgeries were complete. I kept watching for Dr. Garza. He had warned us it would probably take at least four hours, so it shouldn't be much longer. I felt certain he would come out and say that he had been able to get all the tumors, and that all would be well. A short time later he arrived.

The nurse called our names, and Gene and I walked over to where he was standing. I sensed something was very wrong. He shook his head and began to speak.

"I'm so sorry. She was inoperable. I worked for three hours with a laparoscope. I then opened her up, and began cleaning the tumors from her lungs. The lower lobes were covered in little patches of tumors. They were like little grains of sand. I spent two more hours scraping her lung, trying to clean them up. They were too numerous. I finally had to stop."

For a few moments I couldn't think. Everything seemed to crash in on me...I tried to speak, and couldn't. The words kept running through my mind—*too numerous... inoperable...* I couldn't believe what I was hearing. Inoperable meant that without a miracle from God...certain death. Not Marcy! This couldn't be happening!

Not again! I turned and attempted to gather my thoughts.

"Dr. Garza, did you remove the large tumor while you were in?"

Marcy's Story

"No, I didn't. It would have prolonged her recovery, and I want her to have the best quality of life possible for the remaining time she has."

"What are you saying, Dr. Garza? What's the bottom line? How much time do you feel she has?"

Shaking his head he said, "Probably eighteen months at best. Chemotherapy will prolong her life...she should have at least eighteen months with chemotherapy. She should be healed in enough to begin in about three weeks... the sooner the better."

"Where is she now?"

"She's in recovery. She will be there about an hour, and then she will be taken to intensive care. She will probably be there forty-eight hours, and then be taken to a room. Do you want me to break the news to her?"

Gene and I exchanged glances. I knew what he was thinking. Turning, I spoke, "We will wait until she's out of ICU...when she's in her room, we'll tell her then. We appreciate all you've done. We know God has a plan for her life, and He is control of this situation. We had hoped for a better outcome, but we accept this. Thank you again for everything. We know with God's help you did your best."

He smiled, nodded his head, and left. As he walked away, I found myself wishing that I could wake up momentarily and find that this was only a horrible nightmare. Unfortunately, however, this was not a nightmare, it was actually happening.

I had been too shocked for tears. Softly, I began to cry. This had really taken me by surprise. I had had such wonderful peace while waiting for the surgery to be complete. I assumed everything was going well, no big problems... eighteen months--impossible!

Sighing, I dried my eyes and turned to Gene.

"Gene, I guess we should get something to eat. We will need to stay with her as much as they will allow after she awakens. I don't feel much like eating, but guess we should try."

We walked to the cafeteria. It was chicken fried steak day… one of my favorites. We both attempted to eat our steak. We were still too stunned for conversation. I couldn't eat. I drank my coffee…it helped. Gene ate a little. "Tommye, I'm simply not hungry. Let's get something later."

"I agree. Let's go back to the ICU waiting room." We walked slowly back. Forty-five minutes later, they called for the Gene King family. We were going to be allowed to stay with her for fifteen minutes. We scrubbed up inside the door and went into her cubicle.

As we entered, she was laughing and talking to her nurse.

"Hi, Mother, Gene…thought you'd never come. Dr. Garza had an emergency, so I haven't talked to anyone…tell me the news. Am I all beautiful inside now?"

I did not want her to see my despair.

Smiling, I nodded. "Of course… what did you expect? How are you feeling, Honey?"

"Like I've been cut open from one side to the other… sore, sore, sore. How long do I have to stay here in intensive care? I'm ready to get to a room where I can get some rest. Do I really have to stay here for forty-eight hours? I can feel sore in a room. I'd rather be where you all can stay with me."

Her nurse turned, "Marcy, don't be in such a rush. We will take good care of you…besides, your smiling face is good for us, so be happy…it won't be for long."

I told her she had come through the surgery beautifully. I was terrified she was going to ask whether Dr. Garza was able to remove the tumors. She smiled, "In that case, since I'm alive and well, I think I will take a nice long nap."

"Gene and I will be in the waiting room until the next visitation time. We'll see you then." I bent over and kissed her on the cheek, and walked from the room. Gene said his goodbye, and followed me out.

As we walked down the hallway, Gene spoke. "That was close. I just knew she was going to ask if he got everything?"

"Me too! I was trying to decide whether to flat out lie or what? Thank goodness, God took care of the situation. Gene, I need some time alone with God. I'm going to go downstairs to the chapel. I'll be back in a while."

The chapel was empty. I was glad. I had a lot of thinking to do. My mind was filled with chaotic thoughts. The words *"inoperable"* and *"just a matter of time"* kept going around in my head. I sighed, realizing no amount of *"what ifs,"* could answer the numerous questions hammering through my mind.

As a family, we had encountered many storms, and with God's help, we had weathered them all. I felt physically exhausted. My energies were completely spent. For a few minutes, I sat with unfocused eyes attempting to bring my thoughts and emotions under control.

As I sat in the softly lighted chapel, my eyes were drawn to the beautiful cross. I began thinking how much God must have suffered as He sacrificed His son, Jesus, as payment for our sins. Our wonderful heavenly Father had provided the way.

The scriptures John 3:16 and 17, came to mind.

"For God so loved the world that he gave his one and only Son, that whoever believes in him shall not perish but have eternal life.

"For God did not send his Son into the world to condemn the world, but to save the world through Him."

As the scripture states, whoever believes in Him will not perish. If as you read this you are not a Christian, and have never made the choice to accept Christ as your personal Savior, please pray this simple prayer:

Heavenly Father, I confess to you that I have sinned. I believe that Jesus died on the cross as payment for my sins. Right now, in this moment, I accept Jesus as my personal Savior, I accept Your salvation... Your deliverance, in Jesus' name, Amen!.

That's all it takes to become a member of God's family. It's so easy, but sometimes we make it so hard.

Again, I thanked the Lord that Marcy had accepted and believed in Christ as her Savior at an early age. She was His child. We would have to accept what was happening as His plan for her life. Eighteen months seemed like such a little time... so much to be done. Kristine was fifteen. Her mother was not going to live to see her graduate from High School. What would happen to Kristine without her mother? They had attended church together since Kristine had been a small baby. How would Marcy accept the news that she only had eighteen months at the most to live? How could we tell her this? Thoughts kept flooding my mind.

Crying, I turned to my Heavenly Father for comfort.
"Father, I love You. I'm really having trouble absorbing all that's happening. I felt so sure everything was going to be fine.

Marcy's Story

The shock of what the future holds is almost unbearable.

She's been through so much. Father, You tell us in your Word to "cast all of our cares on You because You care for us". I am going to do this...I cannot handle this alone. I felt all was well and now this. Thank you again that You do care for us, and that our concerns are Your concerns. Thank you that You never leave us. Thank you for the five years You have given her.

Please Father, spare her. Guide the doctors as they make choices for her. Comfort us, let us feel Your presence. We need Your comfort as a family. I give You this situation—it's a problem only You can solve. Make Your plan for her known to us. Prepare her heart for what we have to tell her. Let us all glorify You in dealing with her cancer. Your will be done, in Jesus' name I pray, Amen."

I dried my tears knowing that God would see us through. I sat for a short time longer. It was peaceful away from the bustle of the hospital. I did not want to return to the waiting room, but I knew Gene would be waiting. It was going to be a long day and night.

As I stepped out of the elevator and walked toward Gene, he said. "Tommye, I think I will go downstairs and get some coffee. Do you want to go?"

"No, I guess one of us should be here in case there's an emergency. You go ahead."

"Can I bring you something?"

"No thanks, I'm fine. Take your time. I'm going to read awhile.

It helps getting my mind off what's happening. I need to call Brian, Wallace and Mother. I forgot to call, when the news turned out so badly, it just wiped my mind clean. I also need to call Marilyn at school. I'll do this while you are gone. We can go see her again at seven, and ten. I'll just wait here."

After Gene left, I picked up my book to read. I needed more comforting...more time alone with God. As I sat in the waiting room, the thoughts in my head were sad thoughts. I kept reading the same paragraph over and over. It just wasn't sinking in. Sighing, I laid my book aside and closed my eyes.

From past experience, I knew that faith had to be tried and tested, and in the testing, it becomes real in your life. During the times when we feel we are stretched to the limit, totally hemmed in, that's when we need to place our dependence totally on God. Once again, as a family, we would need to enter into God's rest. I opened my bag, and took out my Bible. I needed to read the scriptures in Psalm 37.

"Trust in the Lord and do good."
Psalm 37:3a (NIV)

"Delight yourself in the Lord and he will give you the desire of your heart."
Psalm 37:4 (NIV)"

"Be still in the Lord and wait patiently for him; "
Psalm 37:7a (NIV)

"Wait on the Lord and keep his way. He will exalt you to inherit the land;"
Psalm 37:34a-b (NIV)

"Mark the perfect man, and behold the upright; for the end of that man is peace."
Psalm 37:37

We would have to trust the Lord ...He would meet our needs. We would trust Him for our heart's desires...healing for Marcy.

Marcy's Story

We would need to rest, and wait patiently for him...He was in control... Marcy was in His hands, we would ask for His peace, knowing that He never leaves us. We would trust, delight, rest and wait. We would not be afraid. We would wait in faith. This was the only solution. - God's will, God's solution. I took comfort that God was engineering our circumstances for His glory and our good. We would surrender to His unknown will, and rest in His trustworthiness to see us through. God would be our anchor... we would hold fast. I sat in the ICU waiting room feeling secure that my anchor in God was holding... peace at last.

The elevator doors opened, and Gene and his nephew, Junior, came into the room.

"Look who I ran into at the elevator".

"Hi, Junior, it's so good of you to come". Although he had a lot going on in his life caring for a sick mother, he had an upbeat personality, and brought and laughter wherever he was. Visiting time came and he and Gene went in to see Marcy. A short time later they returned and I went in for a while. She was in a great deal of pain, but alert. I was relieved when visiting time ended... we had gotten through again without her asking about the surgery.

It was dinnertime...I still didn't feel hungry. We decided if we became hungry later, we would get something from the snack cart. Around nine, they came around with a cart with sleeping supplies, towels and washcloths. We were ready for the night.

At ten, we were allowed in for the last visiting time. Once again, she was awake and laughing.

"Mother, I don't want you and Gene spending the night. I'm really fine. It's been such a long day, please go home and get some sleep. I'm getting the best of care...having a nurse watching over me all the time is all I need. I plan on taking something for pain and sleeping all night. Please, you and Gene go home and get some sleep... I promise I'll behave."

"Marcy, we've already gotten our bedding. We plan on staying in the waiting room. If you need us, they will call us."

We kissed her goodnight and returned to the waiting room. We settled in for a long night. I attempted to read until midnight. I couldn't seem to concentrate. Sighing, I put my book aside and prayed for sleep that wouldn't come, and for peace of mind. Both eluded me for endless hours. I sat, feet propped in another chair, with sightless eyes peering into the dim light. Slowly, the night passed. I rested a little and prayed a lot.

At six in the in the morning, when we went in to see Marcy, she was sitting in a rocking chair holding her chest with a pillow laughing and talking to the ICU nurses. During the night, we had been worried that someone would tell her she had been inoperable. I had forgotten to tell them we were waiting until she was in a room.

"Mother, I'm ready to get out of here. When Dr. Garza comes, I'm going to ask him to let me move to a room. I feel entirely too well to be taking up a bed in ICU. They need my bed for someone who's really sick. I can live with my incision pain anywhere."

One of her nurses spoke up! "Marcy, we can't let you leave... you're good for our morale."

Smiling, Marcy answered. "Sorry, when he releases me, I'm gone! Mother, can you stay with me so Gene can go back to work?"

"Of course, honey, but only if it's OK with Dr. Garza. He said forty-eight hours, not sixteen."

Marcy's Story

"Don't worry, Mother, I'll take care of that."

After Dr. Garza saw her, he came to the waiting room to see us. Shaking his head, "She's amazing! Anyone else would be in there writhing in pain, and instead she's in there laughing and talking with the nurses. The nurses want to keep her longer, and she wants to move to a room. I think it will be fine if someone can stay with her for at least twenty-four hours. Can that be arranged?'

"I came prepared to stay."

Turning, Dr. Garza said, "I'll go make the necessary arrangements."

A short time later, she was moved to a room in Dunn Tower. The hospital was full they didn't have anything semi-private available, so they gave her a beautiful private room at a semi-private rate. God was already at work making *"the rough places straight."*

We knew the time had come to explain that she had been inoperable. Marcy sensed something was wrong.

"Why are you two looking like the kiss of death?"

I leaned over and kissed her. "We have something to tell you."
"Gene?"

He shook his head. "You do it."

There were no words that would ease the pain of what I was going to tell her. I stood helplessly looking at her for a moment. I leaned over and put my arms around her.

"Honey, I have to tell you something." I took a deep breath

and turned to face her, the truth on my lips, my heart slamming against my chest. I... I paused to swallow the lump in my throat...I couldn't go on...yet she had to be told. "Dr. Garza did not remove your tumors. He worked for three hours with a laparoscope. He then made your incision. Your lower lobes were covered with little patches of tumors...they were like little grains of sand. He spent two more hours attempting to clean them off. They were too numerous. He simply sewed you up. We are going to have to rely totally on chemotherapy to kill them." As I hugged her, I began to cry.

"Mother," she reached for me and gave me a weak hug, "It will be OK. I beat it before, and with God's help, I'll do it again. Please, Mother, don't cry. It's going to be fine. When do I start my chemo?"

"In about three weeks...as soon as you are healed in. Dr. Kearns has already called Dr. Cotting. She will be working out your treatment. They want to begin as soon as possible. Meanwhile, you have to concentrate on getting strong."

"Hey, you two, don't look so sad. You know my favorite scripture Philippians 4:13, *"I can do all things through Christ who strengthens me."* "I can do this... we'll make it through."

"Honey, since Gene is going to work in a little while, I'm going downstairs for a cup of coffee. You two can have some time alone. I'll be back soon. Son, if anything comes up, I'll keep you posted."

The remainder of the week passed quickly. She was to stay in the hospital a full week, but after four days, she was pleading to go home. The next morning, the minute Dr. Garza came into the room she began smiling.
"Dr. Garza, I really need to get home. Please let me out of here. I'm feeling great...sore but great! My daughter, Kristine, needs me home."

Marcy's Story

Dr. Garza smiled. "Do you have someone to stay with you during the day?"

Marcy turned and looked at me expectantly. "Mother?"

"She's absolutely hopeless. I'll spend the days her, or I can take her to my home and keep her there. Whatever she and Gene want is fine with me. Otherwise, I think we will have to put her in restraints, and tie her to the bed to keep her in the hospital."

"Marcy, we need to put in a catheter for your chemotherapy in two weeks, after you heal a bit. This time we will use a port-a-cath. It is under the skin...much easier to care for. It only needs to be irrigated once a month, your chemo will take care of that for you. How does that sound?"

"It sounds fantastic! You are the nicest!"

"I'll go sign your discharge form. I want to check you in one month... call for an appointment."

"Dr. Garza, thank you for all you've done."

She called Gene, and he said he'd be there in an hour. We packed, and were downstairs in the lobby when he arrived.

Gene and I had agreed we were not going to tell her they had given her only eighteen months to live. We would tell her when the time came and we felt she needed to know. We wanted her to enjoy the next few months to the fullest.

I had spent the week hiding my despair. I had done my crying at night after she had fallen asleep. I knew this was God's plan for her, but it seemed impossible for me to face the fact that in eighteen months she would probably be gone. Knowing her situation was one thing, accepting it was quite another. I prayed constantly for her healing.

"...The fervent prayers of a righteous avails much."
James 5:16

"Pray without ceasing."
1 Thessalonians 5:17

I was certainly doing this. Our church family was constantly lifting her needs in prayers. She was totally convinced God was going to heal her.

Our ride to Conroe was uneventful. She was bubbling over. Dr. Ganza had been amazed at how she had handled her pain. She simply didn't complain…just bit bullet so to speak. She complained the pain medicine made her feel too woozy, so she simple didn't ask for it.… didn't want woozy!

She was going to stay in our house for a week. When she could be alone during the day, she would go home. It would be easier for me to care her this way. Kristine was going to stay with us, too. She wanted to be near her Mother.

At the moment, Brian was doing well. Mother's eyesight was failing rapidly, so I needed to be with them, too. We would have a full house.

Marcy's Story

The Battlefield

CHAPTER EIGHT

It was wonderful being home. Marcy was tired. She went to bed to rest awhile. As I tucked her in, she reached up and hugged me.

"Mother, it's so good to be out of the hospital and be in a real bed. Hospital beds are the pits. Thank you for taking care of me so I could come home."

"Honey, I'm glad we're home, too. I'm thankful you're well enough to be here. Take a nap and we will talk later." I bent over and gave her a kiss.

For some time, Marcy had wanted to re-decorate their home, so as a family, we decided to paint it while she was recuperating. We would attempt to keep it a secret. Over the weekend, her brother-in-law, John, Marilyn, her sister and their sons, Dustin and Brandon, came from Houston. Wallace, Kristine and Gene... everyone worked. This was to be her surprise coming home present. She would be so pleased.
I went to the kitchen to make a pot of coffee. Brian came in and put his arms around me "I'm glad you're home. I missed you."

"I missed you, too. Thank you for being so supportive in my caring for her. I know you need me, too."

Turning to him, "Honey, I have a feeling life is going to get pretty complicated once she begins her chemo. I will be glad when we can see Dr. Cotting so we will know how all this is going to work." In the future, we definitely will be making it one day at a time. "Let's make Nahum 1:7 our promise from God that we will claim."

"The Lord is good, a stronghold in the day of trouble, and He knows those who trust in Him. "

Nahum 1:7

"We'll keep trusting Him to see us through both your illnesses, agreed?"

Brian nodded, "Agreed!"

I walked down the hallway to her room. She was sleeping soundly. As I watched her sleep, my mind was filled with random thoughts. So much was happening. I stared sightlessly looking out the window, seeing nothing. I saw instead, Marcy, as the young woman she had been in another time. A very determined young woman, confident of the future she would have...and now??? So much was happening...so much to cope with, so hard for us to endure. The future looked impossible.

I knew we were to look to God, and by faith go forward while in our adversities that God allowed. We were to respond to then in a right way... view everything as coming from God, no matter what. I knew we were to ask God to reveal His goal for our life in the adversity, and surrender to His unknown will, resting in Him through faith to see us through. I knew what we were to do... faith resting the situation, claiming His peace, and entering into His rest, however, knowing what to do and doing it… two entirely different things. Remaining there, this would be the big problem. I turned and made my way back to the kitchen.

Brian stood up and said, "Hon, I think I'll go take a nap. Why don't you rest awhile, too? Your chair bed couldn't have been that comfortable at the hospital."

Marcy's Story

"You go ahead. I need to do something about lunch. I think I will make some sandwiches."

As I worked, I thought about the storms of life through which I'd already passed. The ones I had made for myself, and the ones that God had allowed.

I knew storms were God's tools, His training period while we were in His classroom. I knew from experience that God once again would demonstrate His faithfulness. He would be our constant companion and protector. During the trial, He would continue to build Christ-like character in each of us, and would be our comforter as we journeyed through. We would give our problems to Him, and it would be up to provide the solution through the storm. Our responsibility once again, would be for us to simply to walk by faith, knowing He was in full control.

The phone rang. It was Dr. Cotting's office. We made an appointment for Marcy, on Tuesday of the following week.

The remainder of the week passed quickly. Marcy rested in bed most of the time. The pain was excruciating ...this was apparent in how she moved. She still would not take pain medicine, and she faced each day with a smile. She was anxious to get home. The old adage was true...*there's no place like home*... especially when you're sick...your own bed feels best! She walked and exercised—always following the doctor's instructions. She wanted to be sure she was healed in enough to start her chemo... this would be her lifeline. Her catheter was healing nicely. It would be wonderful not having to flush it. It only needed to be flushed once a month, and her chemo would take care of that. The only complaining she did was over having to rest so much. She was a doer, and a lot a bed rest simply wasn't her thing. The weekend came, and she and Kristine went home. She was strong enough to be alone. I would take her lunch every day and check on her.

Marcy's Story

We had planned a surprise welcome home party. She was delighted with the party and with the re-decorating job. During the party it was apparent that everyone was silently praising and thanking God that she was alive. We still had our beloved Marcy, and we as a family, with God as our pilot, would help her make her fight for her life. Her desire was to be healed, but if this was not God's plan for her, she hoped to live long enough to see Kristine graduate from high school. She felt if it became necessary, Kristine could manage college without her.

Tuesday came and we were on our way to the oncologist. We didn't have to wait long. We were taken into her office.

As she entered the office, she spoke. "Marcy, I'm so sorry this happened. I spoke to Dr. Kearns and Dr. Garza at length. And we have come up with our plan of attack. You should be healed in enough to begin your chemotherapy in two more weeks. You will come to Methodist Hospital on Sunday afternoon for hydration for twelve hours, and then we will begin your chemotherapy Monday morning. You will have five days of chemotherapy, twenty-four hours a day, and you will complete it on Friday... then hydration until Sunday morning, then home. You will do this every fourth week, and you will be on chemotherapy for life. Dr. Garza will check you on Friday before you enter the hospital to make certain you are healed in enough. If he gives his O.K., we will begin. Do you have any questions?"

Marcy smiled. "No, I think that about covers it all. I can't say I'm excited about this, but we'll manage. Thank you for all you have done. If all goes well, I guess we will be seeing you in two weeks."

When we reached the car, Marcy sighed. "Mother, my life is really going to be a complicated mess, isn't it? Will you come to the hospital with me during my first chemo?"

"Of course, honey, you know I will. You and Brian are going to have to stagger your hospital stays since there is only one of me."

As we entered the traffic, Marcy said, "Put a tape in mother.

Let's have some music on the way home."

"Sounds good to me."

We rode home each with our own thoughts. Again, I felt like crying until I had no tears and scream until I had no sound. The next instant, I felt overwhelmed with anger. *Why Heavenly Father, why?*

The future looked hopeless. As we drove into her driveway I turned. "Honey, I don't know why God is allowing this to happen, but I know for certain that He will see us through. I'll see you in the morning. I love you. Get some rest. I know you must be worn out."

"Thank you, Mother... until tomorrow."

The next two weeks passed quickly. Marcy was getting stronger every day. Sunday morning before she was going into the hospital that afternoon, we asked our Sunday school classes to pray that when thoughts of Marcy crossed their minds, that they would pray she would tolerate the chemotherapy well, and that God would take care of her nausea.

That afternoon the phone rang. "Hi, Mother! We're ready to go. I found the new gowns you left on the table. They are beautiful.

Thank you so much. You are coming in with Gene in the morning?"

Marcy's Story

"Yes! He's picking me up at 4:45 a.m. and I should be in your room by six. I'll help you shower before they start your chemo. Had you rather I go with you this afternoon?"

"No, Mother, I'm fine. Spend tonight in your own bed. I'll see you in the morning... love you!"

"I love you, too."

Gene called that evening after he got home. She's in a semi-private room. It looks like you will be spending the week in a recliner. Try to sleep well tonight. I don't know how much...sleep you will get sitting up. The chair doesn't recline very much. I'll pick you up at 4:45 a.m."
"I'll be ready."

Needless to say, I didn't sleep much that night. I prayed for Marcy—for God to intervene, to heal her. Eighteen months, not enough time...Kristine needed her so much...in fact, we all needed her... she was so special.

I turned off my alarm at 4:15. Didn't want to wake Brian and Mother. I dressed quickly, took my bag and went to the kitchen to watch for Gene. He drove in the driveway, and we were on our way. Traffic was moving well. We drove up to the back entrance to the hospital one hour later.

I went to Marcy's room, and she was nowhere to be found. Her roommate was sound asleep, I went looking for the pantry and coffee.
  She was making a fresh pot.

"Good morning Mother, I took my shower and decided it was coffee time. It's almost ready. Do you want some?"

"Of course. I need at least two cups to be sure I'm alive. How was your night, Honey?"

Marcy's Story

"Fine! Hospital beds are the worst... aside from that, O.K. I'm not really looking forward to today, or for the week for that matter. I know that I don't have a choice... knowing that this is part of God's plan for me--I accept it. Since my roomy is still asleep, let's go to the family room so we won't disturb her. She has a blood clot in her leg they are dissolving. The hospital is full, so she wound up on the chemo floor. She's a Christian. We talked last night."

"Mother, this morning while I was waiting for you, I went over to the education room and brought over these chemotherapy pamphlets to read. It's all pretty much the same as it was five years ago. I have to stay positive—not give in to nausea... mind over body. I have to drink water, eat regardless of how I feel... this helps to keep the nausea down, and exercise. I am going to stand on my favorite scripture... *"I can do all things through Christ."* I know in my heart; God is going to see me through. You and I, plus my IV machine, are going to do a lot of walking. We will be encouragers for others who aren't feeling so well. How does that sound to you?"

Smiling, "I guess you have the plan worked out...let's go for it."

"Did you get any sleep last night?"

"Some! I kept watching the clock to make certain I wasn't oversleeping. I set my alarm, but I've lost the directions to my new clock and I wasn't sure I had done it right. I was awake so I just turned it off. I'll try again next month.

I carried our coffee and she pushed her IV pole to the family room.
We drank our coffee and watched the morning news. A short time later, we returned to her room. She wanted to have her breakfast and her teeth brushed before they came to hang her first bag of chemo.

Marcy's Story

Her roommate was eating when we arrived. Marcy introduced us. I drank coffee while they ate their breakfast.

"Mother, why don't you go to the cafeteria and eat? We're fine."

"I'm not hungry at this point. I will get something later."

A short time later, two nurses brought her chemo. They checked her wristband against the chemo bag, and all was well. The chemo was begun. She would receive the first bag in one hour's time, and after that, three bags over a twenty-four-hour period.

"Mother, I have decided I'm not going to be nauseated. Both our Sunday school classes are praying for me this morning, and I'm going to claim victory in Jesus' name from this minute on. Does that sound like a plan?"

"Absolutely! Let's have our quiet time. Anything special you want me to read?"

"No, you choose."

I turned to Psalms 62, and began reading verse five.

"Find rest, O my soul, in God alone; my hope comes from him. He alone is my rock and my salvation; He is my fortress; I will not be shaken.

My salvation and my honor depend on God. He is my mighty rock, my refuge.

Trust in him at all times, O people, pour out your hearts to him, for God is our refuge."

I finished reading and closed the Bible.

"Honey, we will wait upon God. We will expect deliverance from Him, and once again, we will ask Him to be our constant

Marcy's Story

companion. Do you want to say our prayer?"

"No, you pray... I'll rest."

I reached over and took her hand and prayed;

"Father, we want to tell You we love You and we praise You for Your Word. We thank you that Marcy is well enough to begin her chemotherapy. We ask You to bless her as only You can. Help her body to accept the chemo and not be nauseated. Bless all the doctors, nurses and nursing assistants. Please guide every choice they make on her behalf. Let them be Your choices. As they minister to her, let them see Jesus in us. Father. You tell us in Your Word, "In everything give thanks...". This is hard, but we will praise You for her cancer. We're not able to "Count it all joy" yet, but we'll work on that, too.

We realize that every breath, every heartbeat, every second, every moment, every day is a gift from You, so we praise You. We are going to stand fast, expectantly claiming Your promise to be our refuge, our rock, our strength and our salvation, and we understand the word salvation as to be our deliverance. We know You are faithful to Your Word, and we praise You for this. Again, we pray that Marcy won't be nauseated and that her body will tolerate the chemotherapy so her healing can begin. Bless her roommate, Beverly, heal her... please dissolve her blood clot, so she return home and to work. Help the girls to reflect Your goodness and faithfulness to others as they journey through their illness. Thank you for what You are going to do in their lives, in Jesus I pray, Amen!"

I patted her hand, and kissed her on the forehead. "Honey, with God's help, we can do this. I love you so much. I am so glad God gave me you, Marilyn and Wallace. I truly am blessed. Since we've both been up most of the night, let's to take a nap before lunch. I'm really tired."

Marcy's Story

"Mother, thank you for being here with me this week. Having you here will help me to stay better focused on God, and not on myself. Let's take our nap."

As she closed her eyes, I leaned over looking at her. I was fighting a feeling of helplessness and apprehension… yet a feeling of love and hope. *"Let it all go well Father,"* I thought, *"Please God, let it go well."*

I pushed back my recliner hoping sleep would come. Marcy fell asleep almost immediately. As usual, I sat there wide-eyed. I made a bargain with myself to hide my fears, to give no voice to the doubts that plagued me. I would be strong for her, and with God's help, I would not let her down.

I felt that God had healed her completely, five years ago, so I was really struggling to accept what was happening to her now. The word *inoperable* was continually in my mind. I would have to stay focused on God…not what was happening at this point in time.

The remainder of the week passed quickly. The nurses and nursing assistants were amazed with her. She refused to be nauseated. When she became tired of the bed, she would take her IV pole and we would walk in the halls. She decided we would be Baptist missionaries during our visit each month to the hospital helping others who needed help. During the nights, I sat by her bed in the chair watching her sleep. Sometimes, I would sleep a little, but mostly I prayed.

Friday afternoon Gene picked me up. She had had a good week, and we knew without a doubt, God was honoring prayers from we as a family, and our church family. God had truly met her every need.

Sunday morning came—her hydration was complete. She came home feeling tired and washed out, but triumphant.

Marcy's Story

During the week, I usually went to her house around lunchtime. I took her lunch or helped her warm what she wanted.

She was feeling a little stronger each day.

I called her on Saturday evening. "Honey, you're not going to go to Sunday school and church in the morning, are you? Remember Dr. Cotting said you were to avoid crowds because your immune system is not up to par. We don't want you to catch something."

"Mother, don't be upset... I'm going. This is my life...this is who I am. God is my strength and source. I want to live my life to the fullest, and staying home from one of the things I cherish most, staying home from worshiping Him, is simply not acceptable. Don't worry, I'll be fine."

Tuesday morning the phone rang. "Mother, I'm not feeling too well this morning... I'm having some chest pain, and I can't seem to get my breath. Can you come down?"

"I'll be right there." I hurriedly changed my clothes and ran to the car. When I reached her house, I took one look...her color was terrible... I knew something was terribly wrong. I called Dr. Garza's office and explained we had an emergency. He came on the line almost immediately. I explained she was having chest pain and severe breathing problems. He wanted me to get her to Methodist Hospital as quickly as possible. He said if I felt she was stable to bring her in the car... otherwise to call 911. He would meet us in the emergency room. I helped her to the car, put on the flashing emergency lights, and we started for Houston. On the road, I kept hoping I would find a police car and they would escort me to the hospital, but no such luck. Thirty-five minutes later, I drove up to the emergency room entrance. I had driven eighty-five to ninety all the way. They took her and called Dr. Garza. He had them put on her oxygen and get an x-ray of her lungs. A few minutes later, he hurried into the cubicle.

Marcy's Story

He percussed, finger tapped, her chest. "She has pleural effusion. I want a CT-scan. I've already checked...the earliest they can work her in is one-thirty this afternoon. I think it is probably a pulmonary embolism... a large blood clot. I need the scan to know where to aim the catheter. If it's a clot, it will have to actively be sucked out. She will be put to sleep...it's a painful procedure. For now, we wait for the scan. If her condition gets worse then we'll rethink her treatment. The nurse will call me if there's any change. Meanwhile, I'll go finish seeing my patients."

After he left, I leaned closer and spoke, "I suppose we can only wait—wait and pray. I'm going to call home and activate the prayer group. I called Betty Dozier, and asked her to call the group of friends that had agreed to pray for Marcy, asking them to pray that somehow God would provide a way for the CT scan to be done immediately, and that if it was a blood clot, it would not take her life. I told Betty I would call that evening after the surgery was done. I then called my sister, Marcine, and explained what was happening and asked she and Everett to pray that it would be mucous and not a clot. After the call, I told Marcy to rest...it was going to be a long difficult day. That done, I sat down to wait and pray. I couldn't meet Marcy's eyes... I was afraid of what I would find there. I choked back the tears, refusing to let them overcome me. Forty minutes later, radiology came and took Marcy for her scan. After the scan, Dr. Garza took her to surgery, placed the shunt, and the suction was begun. It was mucous, not a clot. At one-thirty that afternoon, we were taken to a private room... there were no semi-private ones available. God had honored the many prayers being offered for Marcy... I don't know how He had worked it out...but He did. She was resting comfortably in a private room, the procedure done, at the time they were to have taken her for the scan. Our God truly is an awesome God.

The following afternoon, I was reading to her when Betty Dozier and Sherry Bankston walked into the room. They both worked, and yet they had taken off and taken the time to come to Houston to see her. It was just the lift that our flagging spirits needed. We had a wonderful visit and when they were getting ready to leave, they stood at the foot of her bed and sang "Amazing Grace." It was beautiful. Afterwards everyone was silent a few moments except for the sound of our breathing. We knew the Holy Spirit was in our midst…and it was wonderful. We had a prayer and hugged goodbye…thanking God in our hearts for our Christian sisters in Christ. Once again, God had given Marcy the power and strength to overcome. Two days later, she was released from the hospital... all was well.

The next week passed all too quickly and it was time for her next chemo. We again asked our church family for prayers concerning the nausea, and that her body would tolerate the chemo well.

Marcy and I had been praying that God would send her a roommate that needed our help, so we were ready for whatever?

She went in on Sunday, and I rode in with Gene on Monday. When I reached her room, she was drinking coffee. She motioned to me to be quiet. I put down my bag, and she quickly got out of bed and unplugged her IV pole. On the way to the family room, I poured myself a cup of coffee.

"Did you make the coffee?"

"Of course, Mother. I knew you'd be ready for a cup."

"What is your roommate like?"

"Don't really know. She's having a lot of pain... she's in for tests."

"What is she doing on the chemo floor?"

Marcy's Story

"As usual, the hospital is full. She will be here until they find her a room."

"Does she seem nice?"

"Don't know. She came in about ten last night, and the only thing she's said or done is ask for more pain medicine. She seems to know all the four-letter words. Guess we'll meet her at breakfast. Let's walk a little before they begin my chemo."

We walked around the square twice and saw the breakfast trays had come.

"Let's go to the room, Mother. I'm famished. Did you bring your cereal from home? We can share my milk. There's too much for the little bowl of cereal they bring me."

"Yes, I brought my cereal and yes, I will share your milk."

As we walked into the room, her roommate yelled from behind the curtain. "Would you get the damn nurse for me. I need something for pain, and they won't answer my call... I'm damn tired of waiting. Would you push your damn button, and see if they will answer you?"

Marcy looked at me raising her eyebrows and rolling her eyes up in her head, and she whispered, "It looks like we've got our work cut out for us. This may be one very long week. Will you please see about it, Mother?"

"Sure!

I walked to the nurses' station. "Marcy King's roommate needs something for pain."

The nurse was sitting there charting on the computer. She turned and smiled. "She's had all she can have for the time being.

Marcy's Story

We were just in there, and we explained this to her... every four hours."

"I'm sorry. She told us she couldn't get you to answer her call. Marcy and I've been in the family room. Looks as though we are going to have an interesting week."

The nurse smiled and answered, "I'd say so... good luck!"

Turning, I walked back to the room. I walked around the corner to the foot of her bed.

"The nurse said it was too soon. You can only have your pain medicine every four hours. I'm Marcy's mother, Tommye. She said you were in for tests. They are not much fun... I know you will be glad to know what's happening to you. Guess I'll go and eat my cereal. Can I do anything for you?"

"No, I'm fine."

We all ate our breakfast. The minute we finished Marcy said,

"Let's go brush our teeth and then have our quiet time."

I walked to the end of Sara's bed. We are going to have our quiet time. Would you like to join us?"

Sara nodded her head. "Please pull the curtain back so I can see and hear."

I looked at Marcy. "Where do we read today?"

"Mother, share some of God's promises with us. I need some encouragement!"

"O.K. There are some things we need to think about. When God gives us a particular promise, it must fit our need. We must wait patiently being faithful, believing God will fulfill the promise in His time. We need to practice being obedient to God. When we feel God has spoken and given us something to do, we must do it to the best of our ability. With those things in mind, I'll read some promises concerning sickness." I explained this for Sara's benefit.

"But I will restore you to health and heal your wounds, declares the Lord."

Jeremiah 30:24 (NIV)

"Who forgives all your sins and heals all your diseases."

Psalms 103:3

"Heal me, O Lord, I will be healed; save me and I will be saved for you are the one I praise."

Jeremiah 17:14 (NIV)

I smiled and said, "Those are three wonderful promises to incorporate into our daily living. Let's have our morning prayer."

"Father, Thank you for Your Word. It is comforting knowing we have promises to claim when our life seems out of control. Bless Sara! Guide the doctors to the source of her pain. We pray for healing for her. Bless Marcy! This has really been difficult for us as a family, her cancer returning. We were so certain she was healed. I place both girls in Your wonderful loving hands, knowing You have a plan for each of them. Help Marcy not to be nauseated her body tolerate the chemo so she can get a good kill on the cancer cells. Thank you for Your love and patience with us. Help us to clean up our act before You becoming more like Jesus daily, in Jesus' name we pray. Amen! "

Their breakfast came as we closed our prayer... perfect timing.

Marcy's Story

We were off and running. The week had begun, and we quickly settled into our daily routine. Sara joined us each day during our quiet time. All her tests had been negative thus far. I suspected her real problem was drug addiction. Her doctor had cut her off... he wanted to know the source of her problem. Each day she was attempting to clean up her mouth. She no longer yelled four letter words, and she would say *excuse me* or *sorry* when she did.

Marcy and I had been praying all week for her...we were pretty certain she was not a Christian.

On Thursday, when we went to the family room for our morning coffee, we both felt that today was the day.

After their breakfast was over, we had our quiet time. Marcy turned to Sara. "Sara, Mother and I don't know if you are a Christian, whether or not you have accepted Christ as your personal Savior and asked Him into your life. Let me say that without Him, I would not have the courage to face what's happening to me...I simply could not deal with my cancer. There's not any problem that God can't solve. If you can't remember a time in your life when you did this, asked Him to be your Savior, there's no time like the present."

Sara smiled. "I would like that."

Marcy looked at me. "Mother—your turn!"

"Sara, would you pray the sinner's prayer with me. Just repeat what I say."

"Heavenly Father, I confess to you that I have sinned. I believe Jesus died on the cross for my sins...I believe He died as payment for my sins, and right now in this moment, I accept Him as my personal Savior, and I accept Your salvation in Jesus' name, Amen. "

"That's it, Honey, you are now a part of God's family...a child of the King. Now, you can ask Him to help you find solutions to all your problems... and He will."

With tears in her eyes, she thanked us and spoke. "I'm so glad God placed me in your room this week, Marcy. I'm sure you both know that I am on drugs...that's my real problem. With God's help, I'm going to straighten up my life. I really mean it. I've tried everything, and nothing has worked...for the first time, I really feel I can make it."

Marcy and I were on cloud nine the rest of the day. God had sent us someone who needed our help, and He had honored our prayers. It was a great week!

Gene picked me up Friday after he got off work. Once again, God had answered prayers. The nurses were amazed that she was not nauseated. Whenever something was mentioned, we quickly explained that our church family was continually praying for her, and we gave God the glory for honoring all our prayers.

We settled into our every fourth week chemo routine. Marcy was doing wonderfully. The first year passed quickly. She went to church every Sunday she was able. Most of the time, she felt fairly well. They were living free in my rent house. With Gene's income, they could not manage otherwise. I paid all her medical bills, and we were thankful that she was alive.

Brian was having TTP episodes from time to time. When he caught a cold, flu, or anything viral, it would put him in the hospital, and he would be on plasmapheresis treatments. Sometimes he and Marcy were in the hospital at the same time, and I would simply go from one room to the other, so with Mother, Marcy's cancer and Brian's TTP, life was indeed busy.

Frustrated...Yet Standing Firm

CHAPTER NINE

We were well into her second year, and Marcy was holding her own. She did not appear to be losing any ground. Her eighteen months to live were almost over. We now had a private room when she went in for her chemo. Her immune system was gone. It was much better for me. I now had a chair that made into a cot bed, so I did not have to spend my nights in a recliner anymore. She still attended Sunday school and church every Sunday. She informed us it was up to God to keep her well... she needed to be in His house worshiping and praising Him. The whole church marveled at her attitude. People continually came to me and explained how watching her acceptance of her cancer from God's loving hands, was life changing for them... she helped them keep their priorities in order with her courageous attitude.

While in the hospital, the nurses, nursing assistants and all the hospital chaplains came to visit her daily. She was such an up person... they said she was good for their morale.

We gave God the glory for her well-being.

Her eighteen months physical came, and her MRI indicated she was stable. Her tumors did not appear to be growing... not shrinking, but not growing. God was good! Once again, the remainder of the year flew past.

Each month we did her chemo and she was still tolerating it wonderfully. For some reason, her hair was beginning to grow again... even with the chemo. It was still snow white and thin, but she didn't have to wear a turban or wig; this made her very happy.

We had our routine well established. God was continuing to send needy people into our lives each month while in the hospital, and this enabled us to see the good in her situation... in her cancer.

She now had a new oncologist. We had changed over to a net-work doctor, Dr. Paul Holoye. He was wonderful—so kind and caring, so thoughtful. This also took away the mountains of paperwork that I had been having with her medical bills. We had also changed her to St. Luke's Hospital, a net-work hospital and this helped too. Dr. Holoye had increased the Ifex in her chemo. He felt she needed a stronger mix.

Brian and I decided to buy a lot in Lakeway, Texas, near Austin. We wanted to move to the hill country and build a home. Wallace would take Mother, and I would travel to Conroe each month for Marcy's chemo. Brian and Marcy were both stable...life was good.

We found the perfect lot and made an offer. We prayed and left the matter up to God whether or not they would accept it. They did. During the sixteen years Brian and I had been married, we had lived in houses that I had owned before we married. He thought it was time for us to build our own home, and I was excited. We found a builder, had our plans drawn, and at last our dream house began to take shape.

Marcy was doing well. We did her chemo each month, and she was doing wonderfully. She had very little nausea...never threw up, just queasy.

Brian's mother in California had come down with cancer. We drove to California twice that year, to do what we could to help her. On our second trip, Brian, Ben, her husband, and I took her to see her doctor. I went into the examining room with her. She told her doctor that she had decided to stop her chemotherapy,

Marcy's Story

and let the cancer run its course. I was so surprised. She had not discussed this with us. He agreed with her that that he had done everything that was possible, and he felt this was the right choice for her. We left, drove back to Pismo Beach and had dinner. After dinner, we took them home, and Brian and I returned to our motel room. I told him her decision. He too, was shocked. We visited a few more days, said our goodbyes, and drove back to Texas knowing that the next time we would see her alive would probably be in heaven. Brian and his mother were very close, so this had been very difficult for him. A short time later, they called to let us know she had passed away. Brian and I made preparations to drive through for the funeral.

It was Marcy's chemo time. She insisted she would be fine. Her sister, Marilyn, would drive to the hospital each afternoon after school to check on her.

Brian and I left for California. Betty wanted to be cremated, so we had time to drive through. Pam and Harrison, Betty's niece and her husband, owned a ranch in the mountains near Porterville, and they had allotted a beautiful part that over looked the valley for a family cemetery. This was where Betty wanted her ashes buried. The funeral was very special. After it was over, we drove to Blythe to spend some time with Jim, Brian's brother, before returning to Texas.

We were enjoying our visit with Jim one morning when the phone rang. It was Wallace.

"Mother, Marcy went to get her eyes checked yesterday, and the doctor saw fluid behind her right eye. Because of her lung cancer, he was very concerned. He thought this needed to be checked out immediately. She's going to need an MRI. Do you know when you are coming home?"

"I'll talk with Brian—I'm sure it will be O.K. for us to leave

Marcy's Story

later today. You know your sister hates MRI tunnels. Someone need to sit with her while it's being done. Call Vi, she can probably do it."

I glanced over at Brian. He was nodding his head yes. "Brian is nodding his head yes... we will leave this morning. It will take a couple of days. I'll call as soon as we get in."

As Brian and I drove to Texas, I could think of nothing but Marcy. Surely, she couldn't have a brain tumor. She'd been through so much...the words *not a tumor* Lord kept running through my mind.

On the morning of the second day on the road, I turned to Brian. "Honey, I feel good about this. I think this is a false alarm. I don't believe God would allow this to happen...not with everything else she's been through."

"Hon, I hope you're right. As for myself, I have a bad feeling about this. Let's just continue to pray that all is well. This has been a rough year—Mother dying, and now Marcy again. On top of that, they've just closed on their mobile home out by Vi and Wallace Sr... This is certainly not the time for a brain tumor,"

We finally reached Conroe. We called her brother Wallace at the office. He said she should be home anytime. They had done the MRI that morning.

I drove out to the mobile home to wait. They had moved in while we were in California. A short time later, they drove in. I jumped out of my car and ran over and hugged her as she was getting out. Vi had taken her to Houston, and done the MRI with her.

"Are you O.K.?"

"Yes, Mother! The MRI is done. We have a consultation

Marcy's Story

appointment Friday. They will tell us their findings then."

"That's two days...two whole days to wait?"

"I know, Mother. Patience—patience...we have to be patient. The time will pass."

I marveled at how well she was handling this. I felt like a basket case.

Friday finally arrived. I picked her up and we drove to Dr. Holoye's office. He said he had consulted with Dr. Peter Goldenberg, a neurological surgeon in the next office, and he had made an appointment for us to talk with him. He would explain what needed to be done.

As we went next door, my thoughts were whirling. This did not sound good. I quickly filled out the new patient records, and we were taken into his office. A short time later he came in and introduced himself.

"I'm Dr. Goldenberg. Dr. Holoye asked me to consult with him concerning Mrs. King's MRI. I'm sorry, but the news is not good."

Before he continued, a small quiet voice in my heart said, *"It is true ...it's true, she has a brain tumor."*

Turning to Marcy, "You have two lesions—one in the right parietal lobe, located behind her eye near the top of your skull. The second one is located in the left cerebellum... and there is a possible third one located in the right cerebellopontine angle, just above the right auditory canal. I attempted to keep the words he was speaking from penetrating the barrier I had erected to shield myself from the pain of knowing.

Marcy looked at me. I could see the physical discomfort she was feeling was nothing compared to the emotional pain that wracked her soul. I started for her, longing to comfort her, but not knowing what to say. There was terror in both our hearts. For a moment, I had nothing to say...no words of comfort as tears sprang into my eyes. I kept trying to think about what to say to Dr. Goldenberg... for a time, I was speechless.

My tears gave way to anger. My thoughts... once again, everything was out of control. Not one tumor, but two, and a possible third. *God, why you allowing this to happen? We've had enough. How much does she have to go through? We can't do this.* I stopped, attempting to swallow my rising fear. My stomach squeezed into a tight knot.

I turned to Dr. Goldenberg, attempting to calm my chaotic thoughts. "What happens next? We know absolutely nothing about brain lesions. Have you decided on a plan?"

"Yes, I have. First, we will do radiotherapy. After that, there is a procedure called X-knife surgery. We've had some remarkable results with it. It's non-invasive. You've heard of lazier surgery—well, it's similar to that. She will go to outpatient surgery and have a unit affixed to her head. It will screw into both sides of her forehead, also in the back.

This in turn will be attached to the screws on the table. This will keep her head unmovable in a fixed position. The procedure should last about an hour. The machine is computer controlled. We will attempt to kill the tumors. If we are successful, we may have to go in later to remove the debris left behind... we will just have to see. The procedure is not without risks. The large tumor is near the optic nerve. Although we will take every precaution, it could produce blindness. This is what I recommend. We will want to schedule her radiation and then afterwards do the procedure as soon as possible. As far as her body functions are

Marcy's Story

concerned, whatever the tumors take out, we cannot give back. Do you have any questions?"

Marcy looked at me. "Do you have any, Mother?"

"No, none that I can think of now. We will talk to her husband tonight, and we'll call you in the morning. If this is what you think best, then I'm sure we will do it."

Marcy and I stood, shook hands with Dr. Goldenberg, and left. We went down and had the brought from the parking garage. Traffic was heavy. I was glad. I could concentrate on my driving, and not on what we had heard.

I drove on—my heart was still doing a mad dance in my chest. I knew we had to discuss what we had heard.

"Honey, I don't know what to say. It's almost impossible to believe." She was sitting so still she could have been part of the car seat. She was staring ahead with unfocused eyes, too shocked for tears or rage. She appeared more frightened in that moment than I could ever remember.

"Mother, I'm not so frightened for myself as for Kristine...for her future. What's going to happen to her? We both know brain tumors are the end of the line."

"Honey, Kristine will be fine...we as a family will see to that. You must continue to hang in and fight. Once again, we will have to turn this over to God. When fear creeps in, you will have to stand in faith remembering what God has already brought you through. You have fought and won many battles before this one, and you will fight now. You may win or die sweetheart...but fight you must! With God's help, you'll go on."

"Mother, I'm so tired. Sometimes I long to be in the presence of the Lord...but I know Kristine needs me."

For a moment, my courage crawled away in the face of truth. What more could I say? We drove on towards Conroe, each lost in our own thoughts. It was a welcome relief when we reached her house. As she opened the car door I asked, "Do you want me to stay and help you tell Gene and Kristine?"

"No, Mother." She nodded mutely quickly attempting to close the car door before I could see the sheen of tears in her eyes. "I can manage. Thank you for taking me mother...I don't know what I would do without you. I'll call you later."

I drove home with an aching heart. I knew brain tumors even when removed, usually always grew back. She was going to die. The truth as yet was unspeakable. I could think it, know it, and yet not say it. It looked so hopeless. I knew that adversity drew us closer to God, and that in our desperate moments, He would be our Comforter. He understood our struggles, but I could understand Marcy's desire for it to be over, because I feared the worst was yet to come for her.

When I reached home, I sat in the driveway. I knew Brian and Mother were waiting anxiously to know what we'd heard...I knew I had to go inside and tell them. They heard the garage door open. They were in the kitchen waiting by the time I drove into the garage. As I opened the car door Mother asked, "What did you find out?"

Sighing, I answered. "She doesn't have just one—she has two, and a possible third." Finally, the dam broke, and I burst into tears. Brian put his arms around me and held me. I looked up at him, "I'm not sure I can keep doing this. Her body is being destroyed...a little more each day. She has fought so hard and glorified God every step of the way—why does God keep allowing all this? It's almost too much for a mother to bear. I gave her a little pep talk on the way home about how she had to continue the fight. I shouldn't have left her alone...1 failed her. I simply couldn't deal with it. I barely kept it together to drive us home.

She will have radiation again, and then they will do a procedure called X-knife surgery. They attempt to destroy the tumors with a computer-controlled radiotherapy beam. If the doctor misses the tumor near the optic nerve, it can blind her. The one near the auditory canal can cause her to loose what little hearing she has left. I explained that she was already legally deaf, that she read lips. The doctor was amazed about that. The third lesion is not attached to anything vital. The procedure is non-invasive, so she won't have to recover from surgery. After she talks to Gene and Kristine tonight, I will make the arrangements. There's really no choice. I need to go spend some time alone with my Heavenly Father. At this point, I'm all used up."

I walked down the hall to our bedroom and closed the door. I fell on my knees.

"Oh Father, I ask Your forgiveness...1 was bewildered, shocked angry when Dr. Goldenberg told us she had two lesions and a possible third. Father, after all she's been through, it simply didn't make sense. You know how many times my mother has said that Marcy is the best and sweetest person she has ever known in her entire lifetime... and You know mother is ninety-five. Marcy has glorified You throughout her illness, faced the world with a smile, assuring all that You were in total control. We don't understand why all this has happened to her, but we are trusting You to see us through it all. We are asking for Your peace to settle our flagging spirits and our fretful minds. You tell us to bring our burdens to You... we give You this burden... it's too heavy for us to carry. Please strengthen her Father, let her feel Your presence as You comfort her in Jesus' name I pray, Amen!" As I closed my prayer, this scripture came to my mind.

Marcy's Story

"Trust in the Lord with all your heart and do not lean on your own understanding. In all your ways acknowledge him, and he will make your paths straight."

Proverbs 3:5-6 (NIV)

We could not get hung up on the why this was happening, or try to understand it, we would simply have to trust Him to see us through...to make the path straight. I felt better. The time I spent with Him was an island of calm in midst of a sea of terror.

Marcy called later that evening. "Mother, I'm going to have it all. Do you want to make the arrangements, or do you want me to do it?"
"I'll do it...I'll call in the morning. Honey, try to get some rest. Tonight, don't just visualize shrinking the tumors and killing the cancer cells in your lungs, start shrinking your brain tumors, too. Mentally, cut off the blood supply so they can't continue to grow...visualize them shrinking. You have to do everything in your power to fight this. I love you."

Mother, Brian and I all went to bed early that night. We all felt battered and broken. I lay there unable to sleep. I spent the time praying for Marcy and Brian, and for us as a family. At 3:00 AM., I was still too awake to consider sleep. I went to the family room bookshelf, and selected a book. I was hoping and praying that Marcy was getting some sleep. The night seemed endless. Dawn approached slowly and mournfully. Finally, once again, I was able to faith rest the situation. I felt God would use our growth that we would experience with this new trial to make us more effective in our faith... one more river to cross.

Morning dawned and I dressed and went for my morning walk. After my quiet time, I went to the kitchen and quietly cooked breakfast. Mother and Brian appeared, and we ate. I kept watching for nine o'clock to arrive.

I called Dr. Goldenberg's office, and asked them to make the arrangements. We began her radiotherapy three days later. They were doing whole brain radiation. It was pretty much the same... it was very intense. After a few treatments, the top of her head was beginning to burn badly. They gave her a cream to use to make it more comfortable. Her hair was falling out. She never complained...it had to be painful. Every time I looked at her, I wanted to cry...she was so brave. The six weeks came to an end, and it was time for the X-knife surgery.

A week later, we found ourselves in St. Luke's. They affixed the halo in place at six that morning, and the procedure would be done at 3:00 p.m. We were taken to a holding room...it was going to be a long day of waiting. Again, she won the nurses immediately. They marveled that she had been fighting cancer for ten years, and could be so up. One of the nurses asked how she remained so positive with all that was happening to her.

Marcy smiled and responded. "I was given six months to a year to live, and ten years later, I'm still going strong. Every day is a gift and it is infinitely precious. Each day I live, my daughter is one day older. I hope to see her graduate from high school before the good Lord takes me home. I want to see her walk across the stage to receive her high school diploma...and Lord willing, I will."

The time passed quickly. At 2:45, the two doctors came to the holding room. They chatted with us a few minutes. Marcy laughingly explained to the doctors that she had had so much chemo her kidneys were pretty shot, and if it took over an hour, she might have to call a time out and run to the restroom. They smiled and said not to worry. They asked me if I would like to observe, and of course I wanted to watch. I stood behind them for a while. It was interesting. After a time, I quietly returned to the waiting room. I decided I'd rather be praying for God's guidance for accuracy than to watch it myself.

Marcy's Story

About forty minutes later, I heard someone coming. I glanced up and here came Dr. Goldenberg with Marcy on his arm... he was walking with her down the hallway just as though they were making a grand entrance into a ball...him all dressed up in his suit, and her in a hospital gown. I couldn't help but laugh. As I walked over to them, she began laughing, too.

"Mother, they have done two of the lesions. They asked if I needed a break... and of course I did."

I turned to Dr. Goldenberg. "I'll take her."

He smiled, "It's my pleasure to escort her... she's fine."

They made their way on down the hall to the restroom. I followed.
"I'll bring her back when she's done."

He leaned up against the wall outside the door, folding his arms across his chest and said, "I will do it." As I returned to the waiting room, one of the nurses came over. "We insisted on taking her and he insisted on doing it himself."

As I watched one of the medical centers best neurological surgeons leaning on the wall, waiting to escort Marcy back to the procedure room, I silently thanked God for continually providing the best possible people to take care of Marcy. It was a humbling experience. Everyone loved her, and she loved everyone right through her pain and suffering. Most comforting of all, I knew God was continually *"working everything for our good"* as He had promised He would.

A short time later the doctors came to talk to me. It was over and they thought it had gone well. Marcy was getting ready to go home. They had already removed the halo. We were to wait a month and then they would do another MRI to see if the tumors were shrinking. I thanked them for their wonderful care.

Marcy came out a little later. "I'm done! I'm ready for home... it's been a long day."

As we left the medical center, it was peak traffic time. I dreaded it, but I was relieved ...all was well. She still had her eyesight. God was good.

"Mother, did they tell you it will be a month before we know anything?'

"Yes, Honey. It's going to be a longest month ever...but we will manage."

We drove home each in our own thoughts. Traffic moved well—no accidents on the road.

It was nearly seven when I dropped her off. By the time I reached home, I was too tired to eat, I gave mother and Brian the news, took a shower and went to bed.

Fear Not, God is Able

CHAPTER TEN

The month had passed slowly...uneventful. Marcy seemed to be experiencing a weakness on her left side. I was afraid that the tumors were still very much alive and well. We were on our way to Houston for the MRI. I cautioned her about keeping her eyes closed while in the tunnel, but she still dreaded it. I sat at her feet and patted her legs during the shoot.

I had walked to the window and looked at her skull image while it was being done. The big lesion was still very much there. After it was over, they faxed the results to Dr. Goldenberg's office, and we went over to see him. He had gone to look at the MRI, so we waited in his office.

I knew what was coming, I simply didn't want to hear it put into words. In my mind's eye, her cancer loomed like a tall, dark enemy fortress. Once again, with God's help, she would have to breech and attack... once again not giving any ground.

I must have behaved in a normal manner because she didn't notice anything unusual about my behavior, I felt as though we were moving through a bad dream, A little later, the door opened and the doctor came in.

"Marcy, I have good news and bad news. The two small lesions appear to be shrunk. The big lesion is very much there. Usually when a lesion becomes that large, it becomes rock like and it's harder to get a good kill. We are going to need to do a craniotomy and remove the large tumor. I want to operate as quickly as possible."

Marcy's Story

"What will happen if I decide not to have the surgery?"

He sighed and replied, "Without the surgery, the lesion will cause a weakness on your left side. You will not be paralyzed, but you will become so weak that you will be unable to function. You will probably go blind because of the tumor's location, then into a coma, and you will probably live six weeks after you enter into the coma. Dr. Holoye said that you are very healthy, and this will prolong your life. You really don't have a choice. It must be done! We will stop your chemotherapy immediately. The chemo does not reach the brain...that's how brain tumors begin in the first place. We want you as strong as possible for the surgery. Surgery is a must! I want to make the arrangements now. How about it?"

Shaking her head, she answered. "I want to pray and think about it. I'm very tired...perhaps it's time to stop my fight. I'll call you in the morning after I talk to Gene tonight."

"Marcy, you will grow weaker each day on your left side. You will not be able to walk much longer. What the tumor takes out, I cannot give back. I feel it will go fast. Please call me in the morning."

Once again, we were in the car. I could not find the words to let her know my feelings. The silence was so heavy, it seemed deafening. As it prevailed, I still could not give voice to the thoughts running through my mind. She showed an outward calm...sad but calm. I knew we had to discuss what we had heard...tears kept welling up in my eyes...I wasn't sure I could keep from falling apart, and she didn't need this.

"Mother, I'm not really surprised. I knew in my heart things weren't right. I have already been experiencing the weakness he mentioned. When I walk, my left leg seems to drag...I can hardly lift it."

Marcy's Story

The truth was seeping out at last. It was inescapable. She began to cry. I pulled the car onto the shoulder and pulled her into my arms... crying...no words—just tears. A short time later we drove on home. As we turned into her driveway I spoke. "Honey, you really don't have a choice. You must have the surgery."

"I'll think about it, Mother. I'll call you later tonight. I love you... thanks again for everything you do."

I drove home heartsick. As I entered the house, Mother and Brian rushed into the kitchen.
"The two small ones appear to be dead, and the large one has withstood everything...it appears to be untouched. He wants to do an immediate craniotomy to remove it as soon as possible."

Brian shook his head. "I'm not surprised. It seems if it can possibly happen, for both of us, it does. I don't know how much more she can take."

"She's not sure she wants the surgery."

Sighing, Brian asked, "What happens without it?"

"Weakness on one side...unable to walk...blindness...then a coma. She's very healthy. They feel she will probably live six weeks in a coma."

Brian answered. "Did you tell her she's come too far to quit now... she doesn't have a choice?"

"Of course! She's going to call later after she talks to Gene. I'm going to take a shower and go to bed. I've had enough of this day. I didn't sleep much last night... wondering?"
As I was getting out of the shower, the phone rang. "Mother,

Gene came home early. He doesn't want me to have the surgery."

Marcy's Story

"Did you tell him what will happen without it?"

"Yes, he still doesn't want it."

"Marcy, it's your life. You plus your Heavenly Father must make this decision...not Gene. What do you want...you said you wanted to see Kristine graduate...you won't be here if you don't keep fighting."

"Mother, I don't know what I want... I'll call you in the morning."

I walked down the hallway. "Gene doesn't want her to have the surgery."
Brian asked, "Did you tell her she doesn't have a choice?"

"Yes...I think she's tired of trying...I can't talk about it now... it's simply too much! Honey, will you warm you and mother a can of soup? I'm too tired to move."

"Sure!"

After I reached the bedroom, I opened my Bible and it fell open to Psalms 40. I began to read. As I read, some of the scriptures spoke to my heart...I knew God was speaking to my mind... I felt the need to talk to Him.

"Heavenly Father, I praise You that you never fail. I praise You that You are ever faithful. I praise You for our Christian brothers and sisters in Christ, and for their many prayers for Marcy. I ask that You bless their lives and meet their needs.

In verse one, "I waited patiently for the Lord; he turned to me and heard my cry." You have done this over and over, and I praise You.

Verse ten, "I do not hide your righteousness in my heart; I speak of your faithfulness and salvation. I do not conceal your love your truth from the great assembly."

Father, we have not hidden your righteousness and faithfulness in our hearts, just for us, we have declared it to others in the hospital, wherever... Your salvation (deliverance) is too wonderful.

Father, I ask that you heal her totally. Please don't let her suffer paralysis and blindness. Please supply all her needs as You have promised in your Word. Please be Dr. Goldenberg's hands when he operates, combining Your will with his skill. Let him get all the tumor. Please restore the loss she has had from the tumor. Please, Father, don't let her survive as a vegetable.

Verse thirteen, "Be pleased, O Lord to save me; O Lord come quickly to help me."

O Lord, please deliver her...I leave Gene to You...speak to his heart, convince him that she must have the surgery.

Verse sixteen, "But may all who seek you rejoice and be glad in you; may those who love your salvation (deliverance) always say, "The Lord be exalted!"

Verse seventeen, "Yet I am poor and needy; may the Lord think of me. You are my help my deliverer; O my God, do not delay. "

We will magnify you...we how we are poor and needy. Thank you that you promise to be our help and our deliverer. Be in everything for her.

Thank you that you are the God who heals. Thank you for your words of encouragement. I await Your deliverance for her. When I think of all You have done in my life ...in her life, it's too wonderful, I love You. As long as I have breath, I will praise You, in Jesus' name I pray, Amen!"

Marcy's Story

As I closed my prayer, I felt certain that I was going to spend another night longing for sleep... but the next thing I knew it was morning. Mother and Brian were still asleep. I decided to make a quick trip out to Marcy's. She was sitting in the kitchen drinking coffee.

"Honey, I have to call the doctor soon. Have you changed your mind?"

"No, Mother. Gene does not want me to have the surgery."

"Why doesn't he want you to have it? What is the reason he's saying no surgery?"

"He just doesn't want me to have it."

"Marcy, this doesn't make sense. Without it, you are going to die. You have nothing to lose, and everything to gain. Honey, this is carrying submissiveness too far... you don't have to do what he wants... please do what you think God would have you to do... what's best for Kristine. Please reconsider, please! Brian and I have driven you to all your radiation treatments. Your sister, Marilyn and I have done your chemo's with you. Think of all the times she has driven down to the hospital after school during your treatments in peak traffic both ways, paid to park her car, all the flowers and balloons...all the happiness she's brought to us during her visits ...what do you think she would say? Will you call her tonight and see what she thinks...will you do this? Gene has had it made. He has waltzed in here for thirty minutes once a week during your chemo whenever it was convenient... look at all the other husbands that come every day and stay with their wives until bedtime...and he wants you to quit now? Will you talk to your sister about it?"

"No, Mother...Gene said no surgery... I will do what he wants."

I drove home brokenhearted...I couldn't believe she was making this choice. Brian had made coffee. I felt his and Mother's silent questions hammer at me. I felt angry and helpless.

"She's not going to have the surgery. I could not persuade her otherwise. I have to call the doctor. He will think we've all lost it... after all he's done for her... to quit now. Gene doesn't want her to have it... won't give her a reason... just doesn't want her to do it. Can you believe this?'

Brian shook his head. "I'm not surprised. I think Gene is ready for the insurance money."

"You can't be serious!"

Nodding his head he answered, "Oh but I am. How much does he carry on her?"

"I don't have the faintest idea."

Brian sighed. "What other reason could there be...think about it."

"I guess I'll go back out there after breakfast and try again."

Brian replied, "Let me go with you...maybe she will listen to me."
"Sweetheart, I appreciate the offer. I'll go try one more time."

A short time later, I drove out to her house. She was cleaning house. I pitched in and we finished in short order.
"Honey, you know Brian under God's plan is the head of our clan... so to speak, and he feels you should have the surgery. Since Gene is unable to give you a reason for not having it, Brian is afraid it may be the insurance money. Does Gene carry a large amount on you? Do you think Brian could be right? I have to tell

you—after thinking about it, it makes sense to me. What other reason could there be?"

"I don't know Mother. We've never discussed insurance. I've been praying and thinking about it this morning while I worked, and I'm going to talk to Gene again tonight. "

"Good! I need to get home. Mother and Brian don't seem to cook much when I'm not around... I'll go make like a wife and cook today. I love you... call me tonight after you talk."

The day dragged by. I cleaned our house and went grocery shopping...anything to make the time pass. I prayed continually throughout the day for Gene to change his mind. Every time the phone rang my heart hammered in my chest. Finally, she called.

"Mother, Gene doesn't want me to have the surgery. Did you call Dr. Goldenberg?"

"No, I waited for your final decision. I was sure you would change your mind. I'll call in the morning. He'll think we are out of our minds. You are making the worst possible choice. Please honey, please! What about Kristine? Please promise me you will listen in your heart for God's guidance... He's the one we need to make the decision... not Gene."

"Mother, don't go there... I'll talk to you in the morning." I hung up the phone and shared the news with mother and Brian. "On that bit of grim news," I said, "I am going to bed. This day has lasted forever...I'm too tired to sit up. I'll see you in the morning."

I had my prayer time. As I lay waiting for sleep to come, I was struggling with the thought that she had made the choice to die.

The thought was almost impossible to accept. She was really going to die. She was a dream that would never be fulfilled...a beautiful promise that would never be kept. I stared at the ceiling sad and empty crying softly until finally, merciful sleep overtook me.

After breakfast, I called her again. "Honey, I'm getting ready to call Dr. Goldenberg Please tell me you have changed your mind."

"No, Mother, Gene is adamant about this...he doesn't want to discuss it."

This was a replay of yesterday. "O.K.—I'll call the doctor's office and tell them your decision." I hung up the phone crushed by the news. I called Dr. Goldenberg's office and explained to the receptionist that her husband didn't want her to have the surgery. She asked me to stay on the line for a minute.

"This is Dr. Goldenberg. This is really distressing news. Does she fully understand that she has nothing to lose and everything to gain?"

Sighing, I answered. "Yes, she just won't go against his wishes. My husband Brian thinks he's ready for the insurance money. I have to tell you; I don't know what's in his head. Thank you for all you've done. I'm going to keep pleading with her."

"Explain to her again that every day she waits, the tumor will continue to grow and she will experience more weakness on her left side. She won't be walking much longer."

I replied, "I know and she knows...I really don't understand. Thank you again. You have been so special to all of us. I'm praying and hoping that I will be calling soon to schedule the surgery."

The next two weeks passed slowly. Every day Marcy and I had

the same conversation, and every night Gene was still saying no.

After another sleepless night, Brian and I talked over breakfast. He asked, "Don't you have her medical power of attorney to make choices for her? Let's see if we can get her declared mentally incompetent and then you can grant permission for the surgery. We just can't sit here and do nothing. What do you think?"

"I don't know. I'm going out to the mobile home and tell her what we are thinking. I won't be long."

As usual Marcy was in the kitchen drinking coffee. I poured myself a cup and sat down.

"Honey, after much prayer, I've decided I'm going to see an attorney and use your medical power of attorney to force you to have the surgery. I'm going to have you declared incompetent thus I can make the decision for you. I'm sorry...Brian and I feel this is the right thing to do."

She smiled her special smile. "Mother, that won't be necessary. I decided last night I would have the surgery."

"Did Gene change his mind?"

"No, this is my decision. You are right. I have nothing to lose. Will you call and make the arrangements?"

"Of course! I'll go home and call from my phone...I'll put it on my bill...it may take a while. I'll call you as soon as I know something."

I hurried home to make the phone call. "Hi, this is Tommye Hayden, Marcy King's mother. After much prayer and pleading, she's agreed to have the surgery."

Marcy's Story

The receptionist answered. "I knew you were going to call this morning. I've already scheduled it. She's to be at the hospital at 6:00 A.M. Friday. The hospital will call you on Wednesday to pre-admit her. On Friday morning, you will take her directly to the laboratory and get her blood work drawn... we'll take it from there."

Shocked, I answered. "This is awesome how this has all been worked out. God had spoken to both of us." I sighed a sigh of relief...the arrangements were already made. "Thanks again for everything! We'll be seeing you when we get down to the *follow ups*."

As I hung up the phone, Brian came from the bedroom. "She's going to have the surgery. It's going to be Friday. When I called Dr. Goldenberg's office, the receptionist explained she was certain I would be calling and that she had already made the arrangements. When God tells us in His Word that he will go *before us and behind us*. ...He means it."

I spent the remainder of the week cooking and cleaning. I knew I would have to spend several days at the hospital with her after the surgery, and I wanted to leave mother and Brian in good shape.

Brain Lesions... Strong Faith

CHAPTER ELEVEN

Friday dawned and we were on our way to the hospital. Gene dropped us off and he took the car to the parking garage while we checked her into the hospital. Her left side was much weaker. The two weeks of pondering the decision had taken their toll. She was taken to a holding room after her blood work was complete. We changed her into her gown and began the wait. We were both apprehensive... Gene's attitude didn't help... but I knew this was the right choice for her.

I bent over and spoke to her. "Honey, today let's claim Isaiah 54:2 and Isaiah 41 :13 for you."

"When you pass through the waters. I will be with you; and when you pass through the rivers, they will not sweep over you. When you walk through fire, you will not be burned; the flames will not set you ablaze. '

Isaiah 54:2

"For I am the Lord, your God, who takes hold of you right hand and to you, do not fear; I will help you.

Isaiah 41:13

"God has brought you through so much and He will take you through this. Let's have our prayer...they may come for you soon."

"Heavenly Father, we come to You expectantly this morning. Thank you for Your faithfulness to Your Word. We stand on the promises that You will take Marcy through the deep waters of

surgery, and that she does not have to be afraid because You will be holding her and helping her through. Please let her surgery go well. Please let Dr. Goldenberg's hands be Your hands on earth today. Please guide every choice made on her behalf. Bless all the doctors and nurses that will be assisting, and let us be examples of strong faith... that in You, all is well. Thank you for what You are going to do, in Jesus' name I pray, Amen!"

Several amens joined ours. When we opened our eyes, they were waiting to take her to surgery. I bent over and kissed her on the forehead. "I love you honey; God be with you...you are the best and bravest daughter in the whole world. We'll see you in a little while." Gene reached over and patted her on the leg. He was still unhappy about the surgery.

We walked to the waiting room. Her sister Marilyn had arrived. We hugged, but were unable to talk. It was going to be a long morning. The torment was indescribable...like nothing I had ever imagined or experienced before. My faith was flip-flopping around like a leaf in the wind. I shuddered...I had a premonition of disaster. I couldn't keep my mind on the book I was attempting to read. Marilyn appeared to be struggling, too.

I couldn't just sit here waiting, expecting the worst...yet I knew we couldn't leave. If they came looking for us, if the surgery went bad, we had to be here. I had to gain control of my chaotic thoughts. I began quoting scriptures in my mind...words of comfort.

"God is our refuge and strength, ever present help in trouble."
Psalms 46:1 (NIV)

"Peace, I leave with you; my peace I give you. I do not give to you as the world gives. Do not let yow hearts be troubled and do not be afraid."
John 14:27 (NIV)

Marcy's Story

"Let us hold unswervingly to the hope we profess, for he who promised is faithful."

Hebrews 10:23(NIV)

"Wait for the lord; be strong and take heart mad wait for the Lord."

Psalms 27:14 (NIV)

"The Lord is a stronghold in the day of trouble. He knows those who trust in him."

Nahum 1: 7

God's Word began to comfort my heart. After a few minutes my fears began to subside. I knew whatever the outcome, this was God's plan for her life, so I would accept it. I silently thanked God that once again He had given me His peace. I would rest in Him. I went back to reading my book, and this time I could concentrate.

Two hours later Dr. Goldenberg came into the waiting room. I knew something had gone wrong from the way he looked. We stood and hurried towards him.

"The surgery was going well and then she hemorrhaged. I'm not sure how much I was able to get before the hemorrhage, so I don't know what's left. I'm so sorry."

I smiled, "Dr. Goldenberg, we placed her surgery in God's hands, so we know that what happened was in keeping with His plans for her...we know with His help, you did your best, and that's all we can ask for. We'll leave the outcome to Him."

"Marcy will be in recovery about an hour and then they'll take her to ICU. I have no idea how long she'll be there...we will know more after she awakens and we determine the amount of loss the hemorrhage has caused. They will let you see her for a few minutes when she awakens.

Will you be staying...if so, I'll see you after office hours."

I replied, "Yes I came prepared to stay until she's released from the hospital. Thank you for all you've done."

"I'll see you this afternoon."

I sat down filled with despair. He had not been able to remove all of the tumor. I cried out in my mind. *"Oh Father, why...why not all?"* It would come back. If the surgery had been successful, she could have lived a few more years. I was heartsick. My chest was heavy...the cold trembles began. Marcy, my sweet daughter was going to die and it would be a painful debilitating death. I sat there too stunned to speak. I knew that I had to call the family; they were waiting to hear. I choked back the tears refusing to let them overcome me... desperately persuading myself that I could give voice to what must be said. Painfully,
I made my way to the pay phone.

With a knot in my chest, and a lump in my throat, I called Brian...hoping somehow the telling them would make it real. He answered immediately. "Hello!"

"It's me. The surgery is over."

"How did it go?'

"We don't know much yet. She hemorrhaged...he had to close... he's not sure how much he left. He said we'd know more when she awakens. He thinks the hemorrhage will cause more loss on her left side. She's going to be in ICU, so I'll be staying in the waiting room tonight. I'll call you when I know more. Will you call Wallace and tell him the news?'

"Sure, Honey. Don't worry, you try to get some rest...l know you must be exhausted. I love you and miss you, but you are

Marcy's Story

where you are needed most. Call me when you know something."

"I will...love you...you and mother get some rest. It's been a long day for all of us. I'll call you in the morning after the doctor comes."

I sat down to wait. Gene left for home to talk to Kristine. The time ebbed slowly by...the hours crept past. Finally, the 6:00 P.M. visiting time came. I went inside, scrubbed up and went to the desk. "May I see Marcy King?"

The nurse smiled and answered, "Are you Mrs. King's mother? I was going to come for you. She's awake and asking for you. She's in bed four."

"Thank you!"

As I walked in, she smiled. "Mother, this is Angie. She will be my nurse until eleven."

"Hi Angie! Has Dr. Goldenberg been here... did I miss him?"
"Not yet! Angie just gave me a bath. I feel like a new person. How did the surgery go?"

Sighing, I answered, "We don't know." It was amazing that my voice sounded so calm and cool in my ears when inwardly my body felt like it was tying itself in knots. "Dr. Goldenberg said the surgery was going well and you hemorrhaged...he had to close. He said he left some of the tumor. He's not sure how much...he's coming over after office hours... here he is now."

"Good evening, Marcy. How are you feeling?"

She laughed, "I don't know...how I am feeling? I'm not in any pain—no headache...my head feels tight...that's it. You must have done well for me to feel this good this soon."

He smiled, "All your vital signs—in fact everything looks good. Did your mother explain that I wasn't able to get it all?"

Marcy replied, "Yes! What happens now?"

"We wait and see. Can you lift your left arm for me?"

She attempted to lift it. She raised it a couple of inches "It feels like it weighs a ton. That's the best I can do."

Lift your right arm. She lifted it fine. "Lift your left leg for me. She struggled and barely cleared the bed. That's it!"

Dr. Goldenberg sighed. "Well, you definitely are going to need physical therapy. I'll write the order. We won't know much for at least a month. The swelling will have to subside and then we will do an MRI to see where we are in this. You need to stay in ICU for forty-eight hours, and then we will move you to a room."

"Dr. Goldenberg, if I feel as good in the morning as I do right now, I hope you will re-think the forty-eight-hour thing. ICU is for really sick people. I feel fine. Mother will take care of me...O.K.?"

He smiled, "We'll see. Get a good night's rest and we'll discuss it in the morning."

I visited a few minutes longer and visiting time came to an end. I kissed her on the forehead. "I'll see you at ten...you heard the good doctor, get some rest."

I returned to the waiting room and found a sofa to sleep on for the night. I had gotten a pillow, blanket and sheets from ICU. I made my bed, and went to the restroom to wash up. The hospital was good about providing towels and washcloths...I was fixed for

Marcy's Story

the night. At ten, I went in to see her. As usual, she was visiting with her nurses. "Honey, you need to get some rest. It's been a long day for all of us. Please sleep so you can get stronger. They are going to start your physical therapy tomorrow. I've already made my bed. I'm in possession of a big black leather sofa, and I intend to put it to good use. I'll see you in the morning...I love you."

"I love you Mother... look at me... I'm sleeping already."

I went to the waiting room, turned out the lamp by my head and lay down. Husbands, wives, mothers, all were getting ready to keep vigil with their loved ones. I began my usual nighttime prayers and fell asleep. I was emotionally and physically exhausted... totally drained. I was sleeping soundly when someone touched my arm. As I awakened, I glanced at my watch, it was 4:30 A.M. Marcy must have taken a turn for the worse... why else would they be waking me?

The thought made me shudder with foreboding. The next assault was coming and I was not ready. "What's wrong? What's happened?"

"I'm sorry Mrs. Hayden. I didn't mean to frighten you. Mrs. King woke up and she couldn't sleep. She's had her morning bath and would like for you to come and sit with her. It's fine with us if you want to come in."

Relief surged through me... Marcy was fine. My heartbeat began to slow. I was mentally thinking God that all was well.

"Please tell her I'll be there in a few minutes."

A short time later, I tiptoed into ICU and scrubbed up. I walked to Marcy's cubicle and whispered. "Honey, you are supposed to be asleep. What are you doing awake?"

Marcy's Story

She replied, "This is the time Gene and I normally get up... guess my brain clock said it was that time. I slept great! Were you asleep?"

"Yes, it's good she woke me. I was still in the same position that I fell asleep in... if she hadn't awakened me, I would have been paralyzed by morning. I feel good...how do you feel?"

"I'm hungry. They are going to bring me some ice cream and jelly. Are you hungry?"

About that time the nurse came. "I brought some ice cream for you too, Mrs. Hayden, in case you wanted a snack. I know it's been a long night for you."

Marcy smiled and spoke, "How about that, Mother? God is good... I'm alive and all is well. I could be nauseated and sick... instead I'm ready to party... let's party!"

I thanked the nurse for her thoughtfulness, and silently thanked God...my daughter with God's help was incredible. We ate our snacks. After we finished, I asked, "Why don't we have our quiet time? I left my Bible in the waiting room, but we can quote our favorite scriptures. I'll go first."

"...anyone who comes to him must believe he exists, and that he rewards those who earnestly seek him"
Hebrews 11: 6

"Be strong and take heart, all you who hope in the Lord."
Psalms 31:24

"He gives strength to the weary and increases power to the weak."
Isaiah 40:29

"It's your turn."

"You know my favorite, Mother."

"I can do all things through him who strengthens me."
$\qquad\qquad\qquad\qquad\qquad\qquad$ Philippians 4:13

We had our morning prayer after the scriptures. I leaned towards her, "Honey, lift your left arm." She struggled and lifted it a few inches. "Try to lift it five times...a little higher each time". She made it through three. "Lift your right arm five times." This she accomplished easily. "Lift your right leg five times...no problem there...Lift your left leg." She could barely clear the bed. "Not bad! It's a good beginning. Guess we had better wait for the PT person."

The six o'clock visitation time came. Dr. Goldenberg arrived at the same time. The minute he approached the bed Marcy looked at him with this pleading look on her face. "May I please be moved to a room? I'm ready to get out of here...please, please, please? Mother will take care of me...I promise to do every little thing you say."

He sighed. "I had a feeling you were going to ask this. I'd rather you stay here for the next twenty-four hours and just rest."

"I can do that in a room...then Mother will have a place to stay."

He turned to me, "You'll be staying?"

Nodding my head I answered, "Yes!"

"I'll write the orders. You will begin your physical therapy this morning. I'll have them move you after you finish if all goes well. I want to see a lot of improvement before you leave the hospital."

Marcy's Story

"Fine!" She smiled. "You are the nicest and best doctor. I promise, I'll work hard."

As he left the room, he was shaking his head. Visiting time was over.

I leaned over and kissed her, "I'll be in at ten if they haven't moved you. Behave yourself...you got your wish...you're out of here. I'll see you soon. I'm going to the cafeteria and get one of the big pancakes. I'll think about you while I eat every bite. Love you!"

I returned to the waiting room folded my bedding in the event for some reason she wasn't released from ICU. I stowed it and my overnight bag on the table at the end of the sofa. People were really nice about looking after each other's belongings in the waiting room. The woman on the sofa across from me said she'd watch mine, and then I could watch hers while she ate.

I was glad to get away from the floor for a time. I was famished. My pancake was as usual delicious. After I finished my coffee, I returned to the waiting room and had my own quiet time.

> Yesterday, everything had seemed out of control. Today the world seemed much brighter. The Holy Spirit spoke to my mind. *"Peace, I leave with you; my peace I give unto you. I do not give to you as you would give. Do not let your hearts be troubled and do not be afraid." John 14:27. (NIV)*

We as a family would have to keep our focus on God, not what was happening to Marcy, but on God, the One who held the solution to her problems.

A little later they called me. Marcy was being transported to a private room. Dr. Goldenberg had requested one because her immune system was still crashed. We said our goodbyes...the nurses were genuinely sorry to see her go.

Marcy's Story

It was wonderful being in a room...not a waiting room. I put away both our clothes that I had been lugging around, went to the linen cabinet, got my bedding and made my cot bed.

"Honey, do you need anything? I'm going to take a shower and put on fresh clothes. I feel like these have grown to me."

"No, I'm fine. When you're done, we can have our prayer and thank God for all He's doing for me and for our wonderful room... then take a nap. I'm getting sleepy."

"Me, too!"

When I came out of the shower, Marcy smiled, "Mother, you had better make it quick...l can barely keep my eyes open... we have so much to be thankful for."

My sweet wonderful daughter, wanting to thank God for what He was doing in her life...saying and believing she had much to be thankful for, knowing that her death would come soon, I was humbled. I quickly closed my eyes... didn't want her to see the tears forming. For a moment, I could not get past the lump in my throat...I couldn't say the words. Finally, I could speak.

"Heavenly Father, we want to thank you and praise You for Your promise that You will always be with us, and that You will never leave us. We thank You for Your Word that gives us peace, comfort, rest and hope. Thank you that Marcy did so well with the surgery, and that she's out of ICU...for this private room. We give You the praise the glory. Please keep her as only You can, in Jesus' name we pray, Amen!"

I kissed on the forehead and laid down. I didn't expect to sleep. The next thing I knew someone was knocking at the door. The physical therapist came in.

Marcy's Story

"Mrs. King, normally I would have waited until this afternoon for your second therapy session, but I wanted to bring these strips for you to work with, so we'll go ahead and also your mother can learn how to help you. Tomorrow we will try walking. I'll be working with you twice a day and you and your mother can work twice a day.

She had Marcy do arm and leg lifts. She tied the rubber strips to the bed for Marcy to pull and stretch. Her left side was almost unmovable. As usual, Marcy gave it her best. She was breathing hard from the effort.

The therapist patted her. "I think we've done enough for now... you've made a good beginning. Stretch those strips... both arms. This afternoon and tonight before you sleep, do your leg and arm lifts. I'll see you in the morning. Any questions?"

Marcy shook her head no. "I have a long way to go...but with God's help, and your help, I'll make it. I'm not going to give up yet. I have a daughter I want to help finish raising."

After she left, Marcy turned, "I should have had the surgery sooner...I kept thinking Gene would come around. The hemorrhage certainly hasn't helped any...I'm worse than ever. Mother, this is going to take some doing."

Time was her enemy now. It simply would not be enough for her to persevere, with God's help, she would have to prevail.

"Mother, will you sign on to help me with my PT?"

"Of course, I will...you don't even have to ask... you know that!"

The rest of the day was uneventful. We did her exercises and went to bed early... we had some catching upon sleep to do.

Marcy's Story

The next morning after breakfast, Angie (the physical therapist) came with a hemi-walker.

It was a half-walker; Marcy would use it with her right hand.

Her left hand would not hold on to a regular walker.

"Mrs. King, today we walk first... before you become tired."

"O.K... but you have to call me Marcy... agreed?"

Nodding her head Angie smile and replied "Fine, where's your robe?"

"It's in the right closet... Mother's in the left."
She helped her into her robe and out of bed. She put a P.T. belt around her waist and explained how she was to use the hemi-walker. I was to follow behind with a wheel chair in case Marcy became overtired.

We began our terrible journey. As I watched Marcy struggle to make her left leg move, I began to cry. It was taking all the effort she could muster to drag her leg... to even move. I wiped my eyes...I couldn't let her see my tears, or my fears...she was being so brave. I would have to be strong for her. Just as we stepped out the door of her room, her legs buckled and she had to sit down in the wheelchair.

"You did wonderfully, Marcy... I didn't expect you to get to the door... you did great."

She turned the chair in the hallway and rolled her to the bed and we helped her get in.

"Rest a few minutes, then we will do your lifts and stretches with the rubber strips." A short time later she left.

Marcy's Story

The remainder of the week passed slowly. Marcy was doing a little better each day. The week drew to an end. Dr. Goldenberg came to talk to us.

"Marcy, you are well enough to go home, but you need more P.T. so you can function at home alone. I want to transfer you to a re-habilitation hospital in Tomball, Texas. We have cleared it with your insurance. There is no provision in your coverage for physical therapy outside of what has already been done, but they are willing to go along for the time being. They are very good there, and you definitely need more help. We will transfer you by ambulance...can't risk having you fall. How does that sound?"

"Wonderful! My sister Marilyn lives near Tomball, and she can check on me each day after school on her way home. Mother can go home. My stepfather has a blood disorder called T.T.P. At the moment, he's in remission, he's handicapped too, so I'm sure he needs mother. We keep her busy between our two illnesses. He also walks with a walker, so when I get better, we can have our walker walks together. When am I going?"

"This afternoon! I'll make the arrangements. I'll want to see you in two weeks. You will have an MRI and then come to my office...then we'll know where we are with your tumor. Have your mom make the appointment. Be careful, and work hard! Now is the time for you to regain as much mobility as possible."

She smiled, "Thank you for all you've done. You and your staff are really special people. I'll see you in two weeks."

I packed our things and rode with her in the ambulance. I called Brian...he would pick me up at the hospital. I helped her get settled in and left a message for Marilyn at school to stop in on her way home. While I was looking out the window, I saw Brian drive into the parking lot. I kissed her goodbye. "Honey, Brian's here... I'm going to dash so he won't have to try to find

us. I'll be over in a couple of days to spend the day with you. I need to get the house up and running again after being gone all week. I'll call and check on you in the morning. Love you!"
"I love you, Mother, thanks for everything you're doing."

I hurried down to the elevator. Brian was at the information desk when I reached the lobby. I had forgotten to give him the room number.

"Hi, Honey, I'm ready. I saw you drive into the parking lot. I'm ready for home and a bath. I can't wait to sleep in my own bed... what a luxury!"

I filled him in on what was happening. Her whole left side is weak. She's really trying hard...don't know if she can regain enough strength to walk unassisted or not. We'll just have to wait and see."

Hospice

CHAPTER TWELVE

It was wonderful being home. Our new home in Lakeway was moving right along. We had selected the paint, light fixtures, wallpaper, tile, carpet, plumbing fixtures and lifetime Hunter fans during the two weeks she and Gene were deciding about the surgery. It was going to be beautiful.

Her not being able to walk unassisted was really scary. When the house was complete, how could we move if she couldn't be left alone? This was one more very big problem that only God could solve.

I went to the hospital the following day. Marcy was in physical therapy. They sent me down to observe so when she was released, I could continue helping her. She would receive both physical therapy and occupational therapy. They worked with her on a huge bed-like thing for an hour...then on to a room. There she was taught how to get out of a hospital bed alone, walk one step to her bed-side commode, then back to bed. Next, they began teaching her to dress herself with one arm. Then they walked with her for ten minutes, and finally back to her room. She was totally exhausted.

"Mrs. King, we will return this afternoon for more walking. Do your leg and arm lifts after lunch. All of this is very important if you are going to be alone during the day while your husband is at work, and your daughter is at school. We will order you a shower chair so you can shower alone. We want you to be as independent as possible when you leave here."

Marcy's Story

After two weeks she was released. They felt she had made all the progress she could make... the rest would have to come with time.

The following week, I drove her to Houston for the MRI and her doctor's appointment. After reading the MRI, Dr. Goldenberg came to talk with us.

As he entered the room, he spoke. "I'm disappointed ...I left more of your tumor than I thought. If only you hadn't hemorrhaged."

I replied, "We you did your best, and the rest was in our heavenly Father's hands."

He checked her surgery site, and said she was healing nicely. He said he had spoken with Dr. Holoye after looking at the MRI, and they felt it was time for Hospice to begin helping with her care. Now that they had discontinued her chemo, she was eligible. They would also help with her P.T. to help her to function as well as possible for the remainder of her life.

When he mentioned the word Hospice, I sat there stunned. mesmerized. All my senses were instantly obliterated in that moment. Hot tears pricked behind my eyelids. This was not the time to give in to them. Hospice came in when all hope was gone. Drawing a deep breath, I turned. "That will be good... the more help the better."

"Marcy, we will do another MRI in four more weeks... hopefully we'll have a better picture of what's going on. I'll call you when everything is arranged. Meanwhile, keep the physical therapy going. Hospice will be contacting you. Here is a prescription for a wheelchair. You will need one. It will enable you to get out of the house more. I'll see you in one month."

We said our goodbyes and left. As we drove home, we were both silent...dreading to discuss what had been said. There were tears of frustration pricking behind my eyes. I glanced over at her and we stared at each other...tension pulled as tight as a string between us.

"Mother, I guess it's really going to happen. Hospice comes in to help with the dying, right?"

We began to cry. Finally, I took a deep shuddering breath and after what seemed like an eternity, I looked at her and spoke, "Not necessarily, you know we need help. What happens if Brian has another episode? Until school is out for the summer and Kristine's home to help us, this is the perfect solution. We're not going to think dying... we're going to think rehabilitation and help... agreed?"

"If you say so Mother...however, I'm really tired of trying. I'm not sure I can reach my goal to see Kristine graduate. One more year seems forever."

"Well, the good news is we only have to make it one day at a time...and with God's help, we'll keep on keeping on."

"Mother, could you see about my wheelchair tomorrow so I can go to church Sunday?"

"Honey, I'm not sure you are strong enough yet."

"In a wheelchair I am."

"O.K. I'll see about it is the morning."

We reached her mobile home. We had five steps to climb to get inside. They had worked with her in Tomball, teaching her to climb steps, but it was our first attempt to do it alone. Turning I asked, "Do you want to sit in the car and wait for Kristine before we do the steps?"

"Mother, I'm ready for my bed... let's try it."

She used the handrail with her right hand... stepping up with her right leg, and I put my arm around her waist and lifted her, pulling up her left leg at the same time. We were too tired to be attempting this. On the third step she stopped. "Mother, I can't make it."

"Don't even go there... I can't turn you around...if we don't make it, we will fall back down... and we'll both be hurt."

I stepped in front of her and quickly put both my arms around her waist and dragged her up the next step. "Help me Honey, we can't stop now, one more to go." She pulled with her right arm and I dragged and at last, we were on the porch. We fell into a big lawn chair... exhausted but safe.

We rested a few minutes and I took her into the house. She wanted to stay in her chair. I fixed her some cold water and sat down to wait for Kristine. She came a short time later.

"Kristine, your mother's worn out. Let her stay in her chair until your dad gets home. Don't try to move her by yourself... she absolutely mustn't fall. I need to get home. The two doctors are making arrangements for Hospice to come in to help us. In the morning, help your mother to her chair before you leave for school. Marcy, I will be out here around seven. Stay in your chair until I get here. Be careful! Love you!"

I stopped and picked up chicken on the way home. I was too tired to cook. Once again, I gave Brian and mother the news. I told them Hospice would be helping her care. Brian thought that was a good idea.

At our family gatherings, as a family, we rarely mentioned her cancer, but it was never far from our minds.

After we ate, I took a shower and went to bed. Morning came and I was on my way to Marcy's. She was reading her Bible when I arrived.

"Did you get some rest, Mother?"

"I slept like a log… I thought I was too tired to sleep, but the next thing I knew, it was morning. What do you want for breakfast?"

"Scrambled eggs, toast and coffee."

"Done!"

While I was cooking her breakfast, the phone rang.

"Hello!"

"Mrs. King?"
"No, I'm her mother, Tommye."

"I'm with Hospice. I'm calling to make an appointment to evaluate Mrs. King. When would it be convenient?"

"Anytime! We don't have any plans for today."

"How would 10:30 be?"

"Fine! Come ahead!" I gave her directions on how to find us.

"I'll look forward to meeting you both."

Promptly at 10:30, the doorbell rang. I answered it.

Marcy's Story

"Hello!"

"Hello! I'm Linda...a nurse for Hospice."

"I'm Tommye, Marcy's mother. "Won't you come in? This is Marcy."

She did Marcy's evaluation and paper work. "Mrs. King, you meet our criteria to become a Hospice patient. For the time being, we will send a nursing assistant to bathe you every morning. From now on, we will provide your medication. A nurse will come twice a week to check on you...listen to your lungs... do your vital signs, etc. I see your mobile home is split-level. If the three steps to your bedroom prove to be too much, it may be necessary to bring in a hospital bed and place it here in your living room. We will evaluate you weekly and make our recommendations. I don't know who will be coming in the morning, but a nursing assistant will come and begin your care. From now on, when you need anything, you are to call us first. It's been nice meeting you and your mother, and I'll be seeing you."

I replied, "It's nice meeting you too, and thank you for coming."

As I turned back to Marcy I said, "Honey, it's going to be wonderful having some help. Would you like me to run into town and see about your wheelchair?"

"That would be great, Mother."
"Do you need anything...I'll probably be gone about forty minutes."
I'm fine."

"I won't be long."

I drove to the medical supply place and found her a wheelchair.

They would file her Medicare, and I would file her secondary. It was heavier than I expected…I was going to have to grow some new muscles. It would be the answer until she became stronger… I was not in denial about her dying…I had placed her in God's hands, thus her length of days were up to Him.

When I got back to the house she was delighted.

"Now I can go to church Sunday. Thank you so much, Mother."

I prepared her lunch and helped her brush her teeth and dragged her upstairs to her bed. She did pretty well with the steps when she wasn't worn out. I had bought her a close captioned TV.

"Honey, I need to get home. When you wake up after your nap, use your bedside commode. Please don't attempt to walk to the bathroom by yourself. You can watch TV in bed until Kristine gets home, and she can help you downstairs. I love you… I'll see you in the morning."

"Thanks, Mother. I'll see you then. Love you!"

As I drove home, I wondered how they would manage when we moved to Lakeway. God would have to help us do some major problem solving. Having Hospice was certainly a step in the right direction.

Once again, we established our routine. I went out at seven each morning and cooked her breakfast. Brian and mother were cooking their own breakfast whenever they got up. Hospice bathed her, and I came home every day after lunch when she took her nap.

Kristine came home immediately after school every day and took care of her mother until Gene came home. Kristine would do the housework on Saturdays.

Marcy's Story

Sunday morning came and she went to Sunday school and church in her wheelchair. She was delighted to be in God's house. During Sunday school when they were having their prayer request time, she asked her friends to pray that her tumor wouldn't grow... she explained she had hemorrhaged and that the doctor hadn't been able to get all of it, also for God to strengthen her so she could walk better...she wanted her independence back. She explained that she didn't know what the future held for her, but she was well acquainted with the One who held her future.

After church, Beverly Winfree called and said that Marcy's testimony as she asked for prayer that morning, that her courage and faith had made some of them view their lives from a different perspective.

Later that afternoon Dan and Martha Jane Moore, her Sunday school teachers, drove out to the mobile home. Dan and some of the men in her class wanted to build a wheelchair ramp for her. When she called, she was overjoyed to tell me what they were going to do. As we talked, one of God's promises flashed through my mind, *"And my God will supply all our needs according to His riches in glory. "* It was truly so. We hadn't even had time to think about the need for a ramp, and it was going to be done.

The Car Accident...What Next?

CHAPTER THIRTEEN

Time was passing. Marcy was doing well. We walked a little more each day. Her left side was growing stronger. Before too long, she would be able to manage by herself. This was her newest goal...to regain her independence. Brenda, her Hospice person, was truly a treasure.

Once again, the weekend came. Her friends had completed the wheel chair ramp, and it was wonderful. On Saturday morning, Marcy called to tell me the three of them were going to Houston to work on one of Gene's relative's car.

"Honey, I wish you wouldn't go. You will be worn out, and you are doing so well."

"Mother, I want to get out for a while."

"Be sure Gene seat belts you in...remind him that you can't do it. Honey, let me speak to Gene."

He answered the phone. "Son, her left hand still isn't strong enough to fasten the seat belt yet...you will need to belt her in O.K.?"

He replied, "Sure, I'll take care of it."

"One of you call tonight when you get in...have a good day—take care!"

Brian and I had a good day. It was nice not having to go out to

Marcy's Story

Marcy's. I cleaned house. We were dressing to go eat Mexican food when the phone rang.

I answered, "Hello!"

"Tommye, it's Gene."
"Are you home?"

"No, we've had an accident. We are in a parking lot on the right just as you turn on 1960.

Can you pick us up?"

"Is Marcy O.K.?"

"I'm not sure. She's sitting in the wrecker."

"Does she need to go to the hospital...there's one right there... call an ambulance."

"I don't think so...she wants to wait for you. I think she's just shaken up."

"Gene, did you belt her in?"

"Yes! Will you come pick us up?"

"We'll be right there."

The twenty-mile drive to 1960 seemed to take forever. When we drove into the parking lot, we saw the car attached to the wrecker. It looked like an accordion. I had given the car to Marcy for her to commute to her job in Greenspoint... to keep her safe. We drove over to the wrecker and I jumped out and ran over to see Marcy.
  She turned and attempted to talk. The whole left side of her

face was sagging out of control. I knew instantly that she had had a stroke.

"We need to get her to the hospital. She's had a stroke."

Slowly she formed the words. "Mother, I want to go to St. Luke's... I want my doctors."

"Fine! I'm going to call 911 for an ambulance."

Gene walked over. "I don't want her going to the hospital."

I couldn't believe what I was hearing. "Gene, we don't have a choice. Look at her!"

"No, I want her home!"

"Gene, please?"

"Home... will you drive us or not?"

I turned to Brian... "Honey, please do something!"

Brian sighed and spoke, "It's their choice."

Carefully, Marcy formed the words. "Mother, I'll be O.K. Just take me home to bed."

While Brian and Gene were taking her over to our car, I walked over to look at hers. It was easy to see what had happened. She had not been seat belted in. She had been thrown into the dashboard so hard it was crushed in. The windshield was broken where her head had hit...she had probably hit right on her craniotomy...probably causing more hemorrhage...thus the stroke. It was apparent it could have been prevented if only Gene had seat belted her in. I was so angry I couldn't look at him.

Marcy's Story

As we drove back to Conroe, I looked out the window and prayed for Marcy. Tears of frustration were pricking behind my eyes. Time seemed infinitely slowed in this moment. I could not view it dispassionately. We were just beginning to see the light at the end of the tunnel...now this. Her left side appeared to be totally gone. She was toppled over in her seat. Her left side acted as though it had no muscles or bones. I put my head on the back of the seat, and I cried quietly as I placed my arms around her and held her upright. I was heartsick, and at this point, incapable of thought or logic. I raised my head and looked helplessly at Marcy...all I could do was watch as ultimately the new terror unfolded.

"Quietly I turned to Gene." She was not seat belted in...I looked at the car...this is your fault." Words failed... Marcy attempted to speak. Finally, she managed the words, "Mother, it's done."

I remained silent the remainder of the way home. The thought kept running through my mind.

How much Father...how much does she have to go through? She was doing so well...almost recovered enough to be alone... now worse than ever...reduced to this.

We drove into the driveway. Gene took her wheelchair out of the back of the blazer. We put her in and she began to slip out. Kristine and I held her in, and Gene pushed her up the ramp.

It took the three of us to drag her up the three steps to the bed. Her body was totally limp.

"Honey, please go the hospital... you are in bad shape."

"Mother, what could be done...the damage is already done. Just help me into my gown."

Marcy's Story

"Let me stay with you tonight. Brian will pick me up tomorrow when Kristine gets home from school."

Slowly, she answered. "Mother, go rest! I'm O.K. I've had enough of hospitals. Whatever happens... God is with me. You know I don't want anything done to resuscitate me... just let me rest in the Lord. I'll see you in the morning; if not, then I'll see you in the presence of the Lord."

I bent over and kissed her goodbye with an aching heart.

As we drove home, Brian spoke. "I know you feel like you'd like to strangle Gene...but she's right...what's done is done. I honestly don't think much can be done for her at this point."

The next morning, I drove out to see her. I called Hospice and asked Linda, her nurse, to meet me there. She checked her over thoroughly.

"I'm going to call and have her a hospital bed sent out. She won't be able to function without one now. When does she go to see the doctor again?"

"She has an appointment Tuesday morning for her MRI, and we were to see him afterward."

"I'll call his office first thing Monday and see what he wants you to do. Meanwhile, let's you and I bathe her. She needs to stay in bed until she goes to see the doctor. I'm going to try to get her hospital bed here by noon."

I replied, "On Sunday?"

"Our supplier is very good about doing the necessary." We bathed her and made her comfortable. "If you need to get home," Linda said,

Marcy's Story

"Go ahead, I'm going to wait for the bed. I want to see her safe inside the bedrails before I leave."

A short time later I left for home. I was relieved not to have to be occupying the same space as Gene. My forgiveness was pretty used up where he was concerned. I knew I was going to have to do some serious praying about my feelings for him.

Monday came. Kristine called and wanted me to come early to help her with her mother. She was not comfortable taking care of her alone. Marcy looked the same...no better, no worse. Brenda came to bathe her. Linda called and said she had talked to the doctor and explained Marcy's situation. He said just keep her comfortable and wait for her appointment tomorrow. He needed the MRI to view the damage.

She needed to use her bedside commode. She was unable to manage the one step necessary to reach it. Linda said she was going to need round the clock care. I would have to stay the day, and Kristine and Gene would do the rest. She felt I needed to look for someone to help with her care.
Financially, this was going to hurt. I knew I would be the one to pay the salary. Brian and I had put a lot of money in our new house... so things were pretty tight. I decided money was the least of my worries. God had always provided a way, and He would do so now.

Tuesday morning Brenda came early. We bathed Marcy, and she helped me get her into the car. I was anxious to have the MRI done. Today we were going to St. Luke's Tower. They had a new type machine and she would not be enclosed in a tunnel... the machine did the moving.

Afterwards, we went to Dr. Goldenberg's office. He came into the room looking more than a little exasperated...

"It's not good... you have had a stroke. Tell me exactly what has happened."

Marcy looked over at me and nodded her head. I knew she wanted me to give the explanation.

Sighing, I replied. "They drove to Houston this last week end. I specifically asked Gene to seat belt her in ...she couldn't quite fasten it by herself yet. He didn't... he totaled her car and she was thrown into the windshield. She hit so hard she cracked a six-inch hole in it...it looked as though she hit right on top of her surgery. I knew she had either had a stroke or more hemorrhage. I wanted to bring her on to the hospital to you, but Gene refused. That's it! She was walking so well, she was almost ready to be left alone. We've done her PT diligently. Now, she can barely speak...her mouth doesn't want to work. As of this morning, Hospice thinks she will need twenty-four hour a day care. What do you think?"

"I agree. I guess my suggestion would be for you to continue all the exercises she was doing, and hopefully she may be able to regain some of her loss. There's not really much we can do... just wait and see. I'm sorry this happened. I want to do another MRI in six weeks to see how quickly the tumor is going to grow. If you need me for anything, don't hesitate to call me."

"Thank you for everything." Marcy nodded her head and tried to smile in agreement. She had already stopped talking. She was very frustrated that her mouth didn't respond to what her brain was asking it to do.

Once we were in the car I spoke. "Well, it appears we are going to have to start all over again. I'm glad Dr. Goldenberg didn't give up on us. I guess we will take our cue from him. We will have to put aside our fears, gather our courage and make the fight...one more river to cross.

Marcy's Story

"Honey, why didn't Gene seat belt you in?"

Slowly she answered, "Mother...I asked...he just wouldn't do it. I tried, I simply couldn't fasten it.

I reached over and patted her on the leg. "Don't worry, we'll manage somehow." I was attempting to desperately persuade myself that it would work out. My heart was filled with anguish. She looked so pitiful and desolate... huddled in the car seat. I had not remembered to bring a pillow to prop her up. I could see the sheen of tears in her eyes.

While driving towards Conroe, the thought crossed my mind. *Heavenly Father, if someone had to be injured, why her...why not Gene? He knew better...I asked him to belt her in... why her?*

Then the Holy Spirit spoke to my heart through Mark 11:25.

"And when you stand and pray, if you hold anything against anyone, forgive him, so that your Father in heaven may forgive your sins."

Another scripture flashed through my mind... Ephesians 4:26.

"In your anger, do not sin. Do not let the sun go down while you are still angry. "

I knew I had to forgive Gene...I did not want my prayers for Marcy hindered from my being out of fellowship with God. Silently, I breathed a prayer.
"Father, help me to forgive Gene...I know I must. Help me to get over the anger I feel towards him. One part of me would like to strangle him...but with your help, I'll try to put my feelings aside and forgive him, in Jesus' name I pray, Amen."

Once again, we settled back into our routine. Patsy, a woman in her Sunday school class was going to begin coming in for a few hours each day. This would give me more time at home with Brian and mother, and also some time for me. Hopefully, as she improved from her stroke, she might regain some of the use of her left side...only time would tell. Hospice came in every morning and bathed her. The hospice doctor wrote a prescription for a lift recliner chair for her, and I drove to the medical supply and had one sent out. We were hoping that in time, she could get from her bed, to the commode and chair unassisted, but this was not to be. Patsy and I did the days, and Gene was supposed to do the nights. I knew it would be hard for him, working and all, but he and Kristine would have to take turns.

One morning when Brenda and I were bathing her, we notice she had some black and blue spots on her back and legs. I asked her how she was getting injured, where they were coming from.

She explained that most of the time at night when she called Gene to help her, he would not come... so rather than wet her bed, she was dragging herself over to the bedside commode and sometimes she fell on it when trying to sit down.

For a moment I was speechless. "Honey, why haven't you told me this so I could do something about it?"

"Mother, it won't do any good... Gene is Gene."

Brenda spoke up, "I will have to tell my nursing supervisor about this."

That night I called Gene. "Gene, Marcy has bruised spots all over her back and legs. Will you please help her at night? I know you're tired...we all are...you know she can't function without help."

Gene answered, "Can't you hire someone to help at night?"

"Gene, I can hire someone if you can afford the eighty dollars per night they charge, Patsy is all I can afford. You know, I've paid all for her medical bills for the past eleven years. Some of her church friends have helped...they have really been supportive as you well know. If you need help, you and Kristine will have to work it out."

He responded, "Never mind, Tommye...forget I asked."

"Gene, our house in Lakeway is nearly complete. We are planning on moving in October. I have to do this... according to God's plan, after God first, my next responsibility is Brian...then children. Marcy is a grown woman, your responsibility... I've done all I can. I have no idea how this is going to work out... but just know we are moving soon. Maybe some of your sisters can take turns...come up one week at a time to help. I simply don't know."

The next three weeks eked by. Marcy was getting a little stronger. We had to hold her to help her move...but she didn't topple quite so much. We drove to Houston for her MRI. After the MRI, we had an hour to wait before our appointment with Dr. Goldenberg, so I pushed her across the walkway to St. Luke's.

"Where are we going, Mother?"

Laughingly I answered, "I can't tell you...it's a surprise!" We reached the elevator and I pushed the twentieth-floor button. As we left the elevator, the nurses and nursing assistants recognized us. They came rushing up hugging and kissing Marcy. For about five minutes, the whole staff was there loving on her. Marcy was delighted. We explained all that was going on in her life. As we were leaving, the social worker came over to speak to us.

"Thank you for bringing Marcy to see us. She was a shining

light for all of us. We see so much death on this floor...it was always inspiring for us to watch her challenge it every day she was here with us. Please call me and keep us posted on what's going on with her."

I responded, "I will. Thanks again for all the wonderful care all of you gave her. I'll call!"

When we got into the elevator Marcy turned, "Mother, thank you so much for taking me to see my friends...that was the nicest thing you could have done."

"I enjoyed seeing everyone, too."

We made our way back over to the tower, and we were shown into Dr. Goldenberg's office. He came in a short time later.

"I've seen her MRI. The tumor doesn't appear to have grown any. That's good!" Turning to me he asked, "How do you feel about the progress she is making?"

Sighing, I answered. "She's slowly making progress. She's getting easier to handle when she's on her feet...her sense of balance is improving, also she is speaking more clearly. You know her, she's not going to quit, so we will keep on keeping on."

Nodding his head he replied, "If that's the case, I'm going to recommend X-knife surgery one more time. I don't feel we have anything to lose. It will not be considered life saving, it will slow the growth and will give her a little more time. It will improve her quality of life. How do the two of you feel about it?"

I glanced over at Marcy. She was shaking her head yes, and smiling.

"Let's do it!"

Marcy's Story

A week later it was done. Now the wait would begin. Marcy decided we were going to assume that the tumor was dead, so she would have to work doubly hard so she could walk again on her own. Patsy and I did her PT twice daily. Marcy and I didn't discuss it, but we felt we were racing the clock in an attempt to get her walking before Brian and I moved. She was still having bruises...I knew Gene was still doing his thing.

One morning, her left leg was badly discolored and swollen. As I helped her out of bed, she groaned from the pain. "What happened to your leg, Honey? Did you hurt it?"

She answered, sighing, "I hit it on the bedside commode last night. Gene wouldn't get up, and I fell. It really is painful."

"It looks terrible! We'll have Linda look at it today when she comes. I'm afraid you have a blood clot...black is definitely not good...you're circulation must be a mess for it to get so bad so quickly."

Later, Linda came and checked her thoroughly.

I spoke up, "Do you think she has a blood clot?"

Linda nodded. "Probably...I'm going to talk to the doctor. A little later she explained again that Hospice did not do lifesaving procedures, but they did pain management. Marcy would be placed on coumadin in an effort to dissolve the clot, thus making her more comfortable. She would stay in bed three days with her leg elevated until her circulation improved.

As I drove home that afternoon I thought—*another mountain to climb. How many more Lord?*

Summer came. Kristine was out of school. She was taking care of her mother before we all came in the mornings. One morning, as I came through the door, Kristine was helping her mother out of bed. Marcy lost her balance and began to topple over. For a moment, time seemed suspended... everything was in slow motion. We all knew I couldn't reach them in time. Kristine grabbed her mother around her waist, turned her, and she took the fall with her mother landing on top of her. Marcy came through unhurt... Kristine was sore for days. I helped get Marcy to her chair, and told them I had to go to the car for a minute. The minute I was out the door, I began to cry. I was very proud of my granddaughter... she had taken the fall for her mother...placing her mother's needs above her own. After a time, I pulled myself together, and went back inside.

Moving time was drawing near. I was packing some each day. Our garage was a mountain of boxes. We were hauling loads on the weekend when Gene and Kristine were taking care of Marcy.

Every time I thought about moving, I felt as though my heart was being torn in two. How could I leave her? Gene was now taking better care of her during the night. I laughingly had mentioned one morning that all the men in the family had decided that what Gene needed was a good sit down talking time...a reasoning time...of course they were joking...but Gene must have gotten the message...it certainly appeared to have gotten his attention.

Marcy's Story

The Move

CHAPTER FOURTEEN

The next few days were uneventful. Moving day was looming closer and closer. The day before we were moving, I went to Marcy's as usual. Kristine drove into town to run some errands and the minute she was out the door, Marcy began to cry. Putting my arms around her I pulled her to me. "What's wrong, Honey? Are you sad because we're moving?"

"Mother, when Gene was helping me back to bed last night after I had used my bedside commode, he pushed me. I fell and banged my head on the end of the bed. I'm afraid of him, I think he's so tired of all this, he's not thinking clearly...he's ready for me to die. What can I do?"

As I looked closely at her, I could see she was genuinely frightened ...overwhelmed by the emotions that gripped her. A sense of fear and dread swept through me. It went beyond the physical...it was a fear that touched my heart. Each beat was like a loud thunder. Did he want her dead? How could I leave her... she was almost helpless.

Brian and I felt positive that it was God's will for us to move to Lakeway. Marcy's cancer was stable, and brain tumors had not been on the horizon. God had answered so many prayers regarding our house. Our builder had built us a wonderful home. We had not been able to watch the construction as closely as we had wanted, but he had proven extremely trustworthy. He knew about Marcy, and the few times we were able to go check on things, it was apparent that he was not cutting corners. All these thoughts were sweeping through my mind.

Marcy's Story

"Mother, you didn't answer. What can I do?"

Taking a calming breath, "I don't know...I just don't know. I'll talk to Brian when I get home, and then I will talk to Hospice."

Somehow, I made it through the remainder of the day. Time was speeding by. I longed for endless time...unbounded by clock. How could I move...how could I leave? When the time came for me to leave...there was so much I wanted to say...l couldn't seem to find the right words.

"Honey, you know we are moving in the morning. The good thing about keeping the house here, if I need to go between the two houses, as long as Brian stays well, I will. However, I do have to get us moved, O.K.?"

I could see she was using all her resources to keep from crying. Tears brimmed behind her eyes enormous in a face gone white. She was trying to be lighthearted, trying not to show her fear over my leaving... my not being ten minutes away anymore.

I bent over and kissed her. "Our phone is already turned on in Lakeway. I'll call you tonight. Honey, with God's help, we will work this out. Hang in, sweetheart! Hang in! I love you so much. God bless you and keep you."

I hugged her to me. *"Heavenly Father, our hearts are heavy... this is so hard. You know we had no idea that Marcy was going to have brain tumors when we began this house thing, but it's done. Please give us Your peace; comfort us in our separation...please keep her safe. Help Gene to understand he needs to care for her...in sickness and health until death do us part...don't let those be meaningless words. Please speak to his heart... let him take good care of her. Thank you for Your promise in Hebrews 13:6.*

"So we say with confidence, The Lord is my helper;

Marcy's Story

I will not be afraid. What can man do to me?"

Father, we claim safety for her from You...from Your Word. Please work out her life according to Your plan, in Jesus' name I pray, Amen! "

I kissed her goodbye. "I'll call tonight!".

Separated

CHAPTER FIFTEEN

The morning dawned bright and clear...a perfect day for moving. The van came right on time and began loading. It seemed endless...the day wore on. The young man in charge came to me. "We're not going to be able to load and deliver you today. We figure four hours driving time to Lakeway, and it will be four or five hours more before we're through here. We'll have to deliver your furniture first thing in the morning."

I smiled, "Fine! We will drive through tonight. Everything will be ready for you in the morning."

The rest of the day was uneventful...just work-work-work. The van left at 5:30. I vacuumed the house quickly. Wallace would be moving in to care for mother and I didn't want him to have to clean up our mess.

An hour later, we were on the road. It was ten o'clock before we reached the house. We had brought two bunk bed mattresses to sleep on. I tossed them on the living room floor and made them. We showered and fell into bed... too tired to eat. I don't think I moved the entire night. The next morning, I felt paralyzed when I attempted to get up. After quite a struggle, I made it.

The van promptly at 7:30. It was a huge North American Van, and it was filled to the brim. We didn't realize we had accumulated so much in the sixteen years we had been married. Thank goodness the house had four bedrooms and a study... every inch was going to be put to use. I had intended to donate a lot of things to charity, but I had been so busy with Marcy, I had not taken the time.

Marcy's Story

Brian and I had talked on the way to Lakeway the night before. He said if we needed to bring Marcy to live with us for a time, it would be O.K. with him. I had not expected this. It was such a relief knowing we would do this if it became necessary.

After eleven hours of unloading, we were finally in. I marveled at the young men's strength. Our furniture was massive...they didn't even get out of breath. After they left, I called and had a pizza delivered while we showered. Having three showers was great! After we ate, I called to check on Marcy. The phone rang and rang. The more it rang, the more I was convinced that something was terribly wrong. Finally, Marcy's stepmother, Viola, answered. "Hello!"

My reaction was stunned immobility. For a moment, it was agony. Finally, I was able to ask, "Has something happened to Marcy?" I couldn't still the flurry of fear that gripped me.

Viola replied, "Tommye, I can't talk right now...Hospice and a sheriff's deputy are here moving Marcy to our house. Deliberate neglect is a form of abuse... Marcy was afraid to stay here... she made the choice to leave Gene...she's had enough. Hospice was concerned about her welfare. They have already moved her hospital bed. Patsy is here helping. Marcy will stay with us until we can work something out. Call a little later...we were walking out the door when the phone rang. I have to go now. Bye for now."

I waited what seemed like an eternity, and called Vi and Marcy's dad, Wallace, Sr. They lived around the corner from Marcy and Gene in a beautiful doublewide mobile home.

I dialed the number. "It's Tommye...what in the world is happening there?"

"Everything's fine. Marcy is asleep... she was completely worn out."

"Vi, what happened?"

"Marcy didn't want you to know...she was too afraid of Gene to stay there. Don't worry, it will all work out."

"How is Gene taking this," I asked?

"He's pretty upset...that's why the sheriff's department was there. Marcy had to tell them she was willfully leaving the premises...that leaving Gene was her choice. Gene has to learn that he can't mistreat her anymore. For the time being she does not want to see him."

"Vi, I really appreciate what you are doing. You are a very neat lady."
She responded, "Tommye, don't worry...get your house straight and come when you can. She's really fine."

Sighing I replied. "I'll work like crazy...I'll come next week. I have to get a path cleared so Brian can get around on his walker. I'll call tomorrow night and see how things are going. Give her a kiss for me in the morning. Tell Patsy thank you for me. What would we do without our Christian friends? Bye for now!"

I hung up the phone and turned to Brian. "This is incredible...I can't believe it...Marcy has left Gene."

Brian answered, "It was a long time coming... not only was she afraid of him, I feel sure their finances also contributed to this... you know how she felt about Gene spending the money instead of paying their bills. In all the years they have been married, they have both worked, and the tragic part is they don't really have anything to show for it. Security is important to a woman, and she's never had any."

Shaking my head I asked, "What are we going to do? She

won't leave Kristine to come here."

"As usual, Hon," he answered, "We will have to take this one day at a time. You better plan on going back the first of next week. You and Vi will have to work it out somehow."

I sighed, "This is a mess...let's go to bed. Tomorrow has to be better."

While Brian slept late the next morning, I began frantically unpacking boxes. He stayed in bed until almost noon...he was worn out. I made waffles for lunch...they tasted delicious. After we ate, I went back to unpacking.

For the remainder of the week, I called Marcy every other night. I knew she was having a difficult time, leaving Gene, but most of all, leaving Kristine...and then our leaving Conroe. I was comforted by the fact that between Vi, Brenda and Patsy, she was receiving wonderful care. I knew it was going to be too much for Vi doing the night shift because she had her hands full with Marcy's dad...he too was sick. We definitely would have to work something out... but what?

Monday came, and I drove through to Conroe. Vi and I had talked and it was decided that I would come about 8:30 each night and take care of Marcy thus Vi could get some much needed sleep.

One morning as I was leaving Marcy said, "Mother, I have been giving this some serious thought. I want a divorce. I want to give Gene his freedom."

To say that I was surprised would be the understatement of the year. For a moment, I was too shocked to reply. Thinking swiftly I replied, "Honey you can't divorce Gene. He has excellent medical insurance and you have to have insurance. You have

Marcy's Story

cancer...it would be a pre-existing condition. You are like Brian; you are uninsurable. Don't worry about whether or not it's fair to Gene—we have to do what's best for you. The reason you are here is the fact that he wasn't taking care of you, and you were afraid of him. Honey, you would be functioning on your own now if it hadn't been for the car wreck...this could have all been avoided. Have you talked to him since you've been here?"

"No, Mother...what is there to say? Changing the subject, Mother, I need for you to open a checking account for me and also have my disability check directly deposited into it. Put it in your name and mine...when I don't feel well, you can write checks for me. Will you do this? I will help you pay Patsy, and give Vi Mom and Dad some money on my expenses here, O.K.?"

"Sure, Honey...whatever you want. I'll take care of it on my way home. Speaking of home, I need to get moving. I'm going to clean house for Mother and Wallace, and buy Mother's groceries for the month. I'll see you tonight...be good—I love you!"

I had a busy day. I slept a couple of hours that afternoon and talked to Brian. He was doing fine. I told him I would be home in the morning...I would leave from Vi's.

Marcy signed the signature card from the bank. I had made arrangements to mail it in since I was going home early the next morning to Lakeway. Vi and I had decided that as long as Brian was well, I would come every other week and care for Marcy during the night. Once again, we established our routine.

Marcy was now walking to the bathroom for her shower with help. When I was in town, we practiced walking from her bedroom to the living room... she wanted so much to be able to manage by herself.
One evening as I was leaving to go to Marcy, the phone rang.

"Hello!"

Marcy's Story

"Tommye, this is Gene. I need to talk to you."

Surprised I answered, "What about?"

"Marcy's disability check didn't come. Do you know anything about it?"

"Yes, she wanted me to open her an account. It's going to the bank by direct deposit."

"Tommye, I need the money."

"Gene, it's her money. She wants to help with her expenses at Vi Moms. I'll tell her you called."

"I want to see her."

"Fine! I'll tell her you want to see her, Gene, why did you push her down and hurt her head again?"

"I didn't...she fell."

"Well Gene, she sees it differently."

"Tommye, I have one more question. What do you plan to do about Marcy's car?"

I couldn't believe what I was hearing. "What do you mean... you totaled it. She will probably never be able to drive again. I don't see that we have to worry about it."

Gene cleared his throat and answered, "Kristine needs a car?"

"So?"

"If I give you the insurance check, will you help her get a car?"

"Gene, we put a lot of money into our new house...we wanted lower monthly payments. I'll talk to Brian, and I'll talk to Marcy...and I'll think and pray about it. Just keep the insurance check. I'll let you know what I decide. Tell Kristine go see her mother after school tomorrow. Bye!"

I hung up the phone. Life was full of surprises. I couldn't believe that Gene had had the nerve to call me about a car for Kristine. He had pretty well destroyed what was left of Marcy's life... now he wanted a car for Kristine... incredible!

Marcy and I talked late into the night. She still didn't want to see Gene, which was fine with me. We discussed the car issue. As I was getting her ready for the night, she sighed and said, "Mother, if you can afford it, Kristine will need a car. Could you put a couple of thousand with the insurance check and get her one? Otherwise, Gene will just spend the money, and she won't have anything to drive to commute to college. "

"I'll call Donni, and see what he has on the lot. Honey, are you sure you want me to do this? I'll also have to have Brian's approval...even though it's my money. He's the spiritual head of our family under God's plan...so I won't do it without his consent. Meanwhile, let's pray about it."

The remainder of the night was uneventful. The next morning, I called Brian. He agreed that Kristine needed a car for college. He thought I'd better call Donni before the money was spent. Donni was my son, Wallace's best friend. His dad owned Buckalew Chevrolet, and Donni was being groomed to take over when his dad retired. Donni was my verbally adopted son...he was family. I called him and he said he'd look to see what he had that would work. A little later he called...sure enough, God was way ahead of us. He had the perfect car ready for Kristine. I called Wallace and he met me there. It was ideal. I called Kristine and had her meet me after school. She loved the car immediately. She called her dad and he told her the check was already endorsed and to

Marcy's Story

give it to me. I talked with Donni, and said I'd do the papers in the morning.

When I arrived at Marcy's, she was delighted. Kristine had been there...all she could talk about was the car.

Smiling I said, "I'm supposed to do the papers in the morning. I'm going to put it in both yours and Kristine's name, O.K.? I want us to be able to keep control over it."

"Mother, any way you want to do it—I'm grateful to know that she will have transportation for college. It can be from both of us."

"I'll take care of it, Honey."

Kristine and Gene picked up the car the next afternoon. I explained to Kristine the reason I had put the car in hers and her mother's name, if she felt the need to smoke, drink and party in the car, it would simply disappear. She had never done these things, and I didn't want her to start with her new found freedom of owning her own car.

The remainder of the week passed swiftly. The next few weeks were uneventful. Marcy was not showing much improvement. She could still manage to walk to the shower with help, and to her chair, but that was about it. Patsy was going to stop working with Hospice, and the Hospice volunteers we would have to manage. I would continue to come every other week, and Vi would do the rest. Hospice had suggested that we use diapers on Marcy at night, and she could use her bedside commode during the day. That way, Vi could get more rest at night.

The following week, Tara, the social worker for Hospice called me in Austin. "Mrs. Hayden, when you come next week, we need to evaluate Mrs. King's options. When would be a good time for you?"

"Any morning, I'll just stay over."

"Let's try for Tuesday. I'll check with Mrs. Dodd, and see if this is convenient. If it's not, I'll call you...if you don't hear from me, I will see you Tuesday morning."

"Fine! I'll see you then."

All my weeks in Austin flew by...in Conroe, an eternity. The drive was getting longer and longer. I usually left food cooked, and Brian warmed whatever he wanted in the microwave.

Tuesday morning came, and we were all in our places...Marcy in her wheelchair, Linda, Vi, Tara and myself. Tara explained that Marcy's case manager from MetLife had called and suggested that they wanted Marcy placed in a health care facility...one with a skilled nursing unit. They felt that this was in her best interest and although there was no coverage for this in her policy, they would pay for it. If she improved, then we could talk about moving her home. As she finished the explanation, she asked, "What do you think about this?"

I replied, "Health care facility… skilled nursing unit...meaning what? Are we talking about placing her in a nursing home?"

Tara nodded her head and answered, "Yes, that's what they want."

My teeth were clenched so hard my jaw ached. Some semblance of organized thought finally began to sweep through my mind... this was a terrible moment. My eyes burned bright and dry...a nursing home...never! I took a deep breath and spoke, "I don't know how Vi feels about this, but I am certainly not in favor of doing this. I don't want her in a nursing home...ever...just give

Marcy's Story

me some time, I'll make some different arrangements for her."

"Mrs. Hayden, I don't feel you really have a choice. When an insurance company makes a recommendation, a suggestion, this is what they want, they expect us to act on it. If you want Mrs. King to continue to receive the excellent care she has had... then I feel we must give this a try."

I glanced over at Marcy...I knew in an instant she was struggling to hold back the tears that had gathered in her eyes. I turned to Vi, "What do you think?"

She answered," If this is what they want, I guess we give it a try."

Tara looked over at Marcy, "Mrs. King, Brenda will still be the nursing assistant assigned to you. She will come to whatever health care facility you choose, Linda will be your nurse, she will come twice a week to check on you, and Hospice will still be managing your care. Everything will remain pretty much the same, except you'll be eating and sleeping in a different place."

With a sinking heart, I realized that perhaps I should be happy that MetLife was willing to do this—but Marcy was too young to be placed in a nursing home. Through the years, I had taken musical ensembles to various nursing homes to sing for the seniors in an attempt to brighten their days. They enjoyed hearing and singing the old familiar hymns. For Marcy to be placed in a facility where ninety percent of the patients were Alzheimer's patients... this was unthinkable.

I looked over at Marcy, and attempted to choke down the lump in my throat. I felt tears coming into my eyes, as my anger subsided into a dull ache of disappointment and heartache.

"Honey, I guess for the time being, we have to do this."

Marcy's Story

Marcy nodded her head and spoke, "I understand. I guess if I can have Brenda and Linda, I can survive."

"Mrs. Hayden, you and Mrs. Dodd can choose the facility...the only requirement, it must have a skilled nursing unit. There are four homes in this vicinity, but I believe the one in the Woodlands is the only one that has a skilled nursing unit. I would suggest your going to look at the homes, and checking about the skilled nursing unit. Let me know your decision, and I'll make the arrangements. We will move her by ambulance. That's all I have for you at this time. Do you have any questions?"

I shook my head no. We stood and Vi and I walked them to the door.

We thanked them for all they were doing for Marcy.

Vi turned, "It's lunch time, take Marcy to the snack bar and I'll make some sandwiches. Stay and have lunch with us."

"Thanks anyway Vi, I need to get home. Mother's out of food."

I bent over and put my arms around Marcy. I did not voice the troubled thoughts that crowded my mind.

"Honey, this has really taken us by surprise. None of us expected this...I guess the bottom line is that we will need to view this as God's plan for you at this point in time. Nursing homes cost around four thousand a month, and if they are willing to pay for it because they feel it's in your best interest, I guess we do it...no choice. Honey, when Tara presented this, when I was struggling not to burst into tears, Psalms 27:14 flashed through my mind."

"Wait for the Lord, be strong let your heart take courage; yes, wait for the Lord."

Marcy's Story

"Honey, I guess we as a family are about to become nursing home missionaries. We will have to be strong and courageous in the Lord. Sweetheart, you have always moved onward, no matter what the odds were, so you can't stop now. We are all so proud of you...I love you—you'll see, we'll work it out."

I kissed her and then hugged Vi. "If you and her dad hadn't taken Marcy in when the Gene thing happened, I don't know what we would have done. Thank you...I'll see you gals tonight. Bye!"

I rushed out to the car. I barely got the car door open before I began to cry. Now I was alone. I wanted to scream, yell and cry all at once. Heartbrokenly, I sobbed...Marcy in a nursing home—I cried out in anguish! *"How much more Lord, she's been through so much...how much more?"*

I stopped on the way home and bought food for Mother. I didn't feel like eating.

"Mother, Met Life wants Marcy to go to a nursing home. They feel she needs to be where there is a skilled nursing unit. It seems we don't have a choice. I don't know if I can do this... but I guess we must. I'm going to take a shower and rest until bedtime after I talk to Brian. I'll see you in the morning. I love you! Goodnight!"

I called Vi to check on how Marcy was handling the catastrophic news concerning the move. They had just finished watching a movie. It was a comedy, and the three of them had laughed so much their sides were still aching. She said it had been a wonderful evening.

As I sat for a few moments thinking, I realized that without Vi, Mom and Wallace, Sr., all of this mess would have been unbearable. They had given Marcy a home and loving care when there was no one else to do it...I would always be grateful.

After my shower, I went to bed. The silence screamed...I closed my eyes attempting to force my mind to blankness. I prayed for the forgetfulness of sleep... finally it came.

The Nursing Home

CHAPTER SIXTEEN

I spent the next morning looking at nursing homes. Finally, after much prayer, I made the choice for her. I called Tara, and she made the arrangements. Marcy was transported by ambulance. Her semi-private room was nice. At the moment, the other bed was empty, so this gave her more room. She was given the first room off the big family room, thus we didn't have to go down the long halls seeing all the Alzheimer's patients. Gene and Kristine volunteered to move her lift chair, bedside commode and TV in Gene's truck. Gene appeared to be happy that Marcy was now in a place where he could see her whether she wanted it or not, I signed all the paperwork and she was in. I spent the remainder of the day putting her things away. Hospice came and set up her chart with her medication list. everything was done. It was time for me to leave...but how could I leave her...she was so alone.

"Marcy, I need to go home. I'm worn out. Honey, I know this seems impossible and I have to admit this is not what I wanted for you, but we don't have a choice. With God's help, we can make this work. Two scriptures are coming to my mind."

"I will listen to what God the Lord will say; he promises peace to his people, his saints..."
Psalms 85:8

"And the peace of God, which transcends all understanding will guard your hearts and your minds in Christ Jesus.
Philippians 4:7 (NIV)

"We will ask for His peace in this matter. I'll be here first thing in the morning. Let's have our night time prayer."

Heavenly Father, once again, You have given Marcy a mountain to climb. We praise You that You promised You would never leave us, so we claim this for her. Let her feel Your comforting presence. Help her to make new friends, and be Your Light here in this place, in Jesus' name I pray, Amen!"

"Honey, let me push you to the dining room for your evening meal...you can check out the food, OK? The nursing assistant will take you back to your room after you are done. "

"Let's do it Mother."

The dining room was lovely. I asked one of the nursing assistants if she knew where Mrs. King was to sit, and she took us to her table. Another woman was already there. We introduced ourselves. I explained Marcy was hearing impaired, and that she would need to face her so Marcy could read her lips in order for them to talk. I had also had them put a sign over her bed... so everything was covered.

I bent over and hugged Marcy. "I'm going now. I'll be here first thing in the morning. You get some rest...you have to be exhausted, too. I love you."

Further words eluded me. I turned my face aside so she could not see the tears that started in my eyes. I felt as though my heart was going to break.

Bravely, she took a deep breath and attempted a smile. She lowered her head letting her lashes fall in an attempt to hide the anguish in her eyes. "I love you too, Mother, I'll see you in the morning. Thank you, Mother!"

I hurriedly left the dining room. I wanted to reach my car before I began to cry. Surprisingly, I didn't cry...instead my eyes

Marcy's Story

burned from the dryness of unshed tears. I automatically drove to the house and called Brian. We didn't talk long... I was still having difficulty keeping it together. Mother was in her room. I talked to her for a few minutes and then went to the shower. I didn't feel like eating, so I went to my room and closed the door.

I was determined not to give in to the anguish and rage that was sweeping through me. I quelled the urge to scream and I fought for control, but the flood of tears came. I cried until there were no more tears left—then I slept.

The next thing I knew, it was morning. I dressed and went to the kitchen to cook our breakfast. After we ate, I put the dishes in the dishwasher and left for the nursing home. I stopped at the service station and bought us some cappuccino coffee. Marcy was sitting in her chair.

As I handed her the coffee I said, "Hi, Honey, it's party time. How was your night?"

She shook her head and answered, "Not good. I turned on my light and after forty-five minutes, they finally answered it. It seems they only have two aides, and they don't have time to help me to my bedside commode. They keep everyone here in diapers here around the clock, and they want this for me. Mother, I'm not incontinent, I don't want to wear diapers. Will you please talk to them?"

"Sure, I'll go see about it now."

I walked to the nurse's station and talked to the nurse explaining the problem. She was very sympathetic but she explained they did not have the help to provide assistance for Marcy to help her to her commode night or day. I walked to the director's office and she too explained that this was typical of all nursing homes. With a sinking heart I walked back to Marcy's room.

Marcy's Story

"Honey, I'm sorry. They don't make any exceptions. I guess we have to work on your physical therapy, and see if we can't get you able to do it on your own. For the time being, I guess you will have to go into diapers. This is one thing I didn't think to ask about."

Brenda, the Hospice nursing assistant, came in about that time. "Good morning ladies, how are you?"

I shook my head and replied, "Not too good. We've just found out Marcy is going to have to wear diapers... they don't have the time nor the help to get her to her commode when she needs it. That is bad! I spoke to all the ones in authority, and that's simply how it is."

Brenda turned to Marcy and smiled. "Marcy, it will work out. I will be here early each morning to bathe you, and when your mom is here, she can help during the day...we will do the best we can where this in concerned. Meantime, how about a whirlpool bath today? I have signed you up for Tuesday and Thursday. The rest of the time, we will give you a shower here in your bathroom. Let's get started."

Marcy said she felt like a new person when they returned. I had changed her bed and laid out her clothes for the day. After Brenda left, we visited, had our quiet time and watched TV. We did her PT, and walked with her hemi walker. She could barely move. When lunchtime came, I put her in her wheelchair and took her to the dining room. She would walk herself back to the room when she was finished in the wheelchair. This would help strengthen her legs. After lunch, everyone in the nursing home was put to bed for two hours for a nap... without exception.

After naptime, some of the churches came and gave a devotional for with those who were able to attend. They sometimes brought entertainers from Houston. Some of the residents did ceramics. They played BINGO twice a week, and a group of ladies from a service league came monthly and gave a big birthday party for all the people that had birthdays that month. In all, the activities director did a good job of providing entertainment for those who were able to attend.

Friday morning came, and we went through our usual routine. I would be leaving for Austin after I took her to lunch. We weren't able to talk much that morning. My leaving was hanging heavily on both our hearts. I would spend the following week with Brian, and then return to Conroe...I would continue the every other week thing for the time being as long as Brian stayed well.

The morning passed quickly and it was time for lunch. "Honey, I need to get on the road...otherwise I will get into Austin during peak traffic time and it takes forever to get home when that happens. I hate the thought of leaving you, but I must go to Brian. He hasn't been feeling too well lately. I know we can't talk since you can't hear over the phone, but I will check on you through Hospice. I'll be back in a week just as we've been doing. I love you so much... you are the bravest person I know. With God's help, you can do this. I'm going to take you to the dining room now."

"I know you have to go, she choked out... I don't know if I can do this without you, Mother, but I'll do my best. I love you!" I pushed her to the dining room kissed her, and with a sinking heart hurried away.

As I reached my car, the thunder of my heart was nearly suffocating. I fought for control fighting the urge to scream, yet determined not to give way to all the churning terrible thoughts that crowded my mind. Finally, I collapsed against the steering wheel... unable to hold back the tears any longer. It was my hope that as they began to know her, they would somehow give her better care...she was so alone. She had always been a people person...always so giving...her infectious laughter was contagious, and had brought gladness and joy wherever she found herself, always making the best of every situation. I breathed a prayer, *"Oh God, comfort her... I know this of the big plan You have for her...but it seems impossible. Please care for her as only You can, and give me a safe journey home, in Jesus' name I pray, Amen!"*

I put in a Bill Gaither CD, and I was on my way.

The Fall

CHAPTER SEVENTEEN

The trip to Lakeway was uneventful. It was good being home. I called every other night to check on Marcy. She was lonely, but fine. Gene was going by to see her a couple of times a week on his way home, so this helped. Once again, we established our routine. Brian was not feeling too well…his platelets were low but hanging in.

I returned to Conroe every other week and took care of Marcy. Vi Mom and Marcy's Dad usually went once a week, Marilyn continued her Saturday visits, and with all the activities time was passing. Her care was appalling, but that didn't seem to change in spite of all my pleas for more help for her.

I made reservations for the conference room for Thanksgiving, and we cooked all her favorite dishes and took Thanksgiving to her. She was delighted. It was a good day…everyone enjoyed it…the whole family came. We invited the nurses and nursing assistants to stop by and fix their plates. Late that afternoon, Marcy returned to her room tired but triumphant.

The weeks passed quickly. Gene and Kristine wanted to take Marcy home on Christmas day for a quiet Christmas. This worked for me…Brian had told me he didn't feel like making the trip to Conroe, so problem solved. Mother went home with my sister, Marcine, Wallace went to Donni, Leesa and Danna's, Marilyn cooked for the Davlins'…everyone had a place. Brian and I enjoyed having quality time alone together.

Tuesday morning dawned, and I awakened with a feeling that

something was wrong. I didn't understand the strange dread that filled me...it was like a premonition that something had happened. Hospice called me...it seems Gene had let Marcy fall Christmas day when she was going from the bedside commode to the chair when she was getting ready to go back to the nursing home. She was having excruciating lower back pain and they needed to run some tests.

I drove through early the next morning, and rode in the ambulance to the orthopedic surgeon with Marcy. Her spine was fractured...a fractured vertebrae. She was to have six weeks total bed rest on her back, and hopefully it would mend properly... otherwise she would have severe pain the remainder of her life. They intended to keep her heavily sedated for a few days so the healing process could begin.

I returned to Lakeway the next afternoon. Marcy informed me she planned on sleeping the month away while she healed and that she had rather I be here with her when she was quote, *up and at 'em!* There wasn't much I could do for her so once again I was on the road.

The next few weeks passed. Marcy was still in severe pain. She could no longer walk. The six weeks in bed had finished that. She now had to be lifted from the bed to her chair and she could only stay in her chair for a short time before the pain racked her body and she would have to be returned to bed. She could no longer turn herself over… she had to lie there until someone came to answer her light and help her. Sometimes it took thirty to forty-five minutes. It was almost more than I could endure seeing her as she was.

Dan and Martha Jane took the Sunday School class to her room several times and they had the lesson in her room. Her dear sister in Christ, Lynn Webb, came every week always bringing her something to cheer her and her sister Marilyn still came on Saturdays. Our church family was totally supportive always

Marcy's Story

bringing flowers, stuffed animals, and inspirational books. If only the pain were not so severe. It became harder to leave her each time I came.

The months crept by. It was time for Kristine's graduation. God had granted Marcy her heart's desire, her wish to see Kristine graduate. Hospice made arrangements for Marcy to be taken to Huntsville by ambulance to see Kristine cross the stage for her diploma. This was their gift to Marcy. I was concerned that she wouldn't be able to bear the pain of sitting in her wheelchair watching, but God honored our prayers and she was fine. When we returned to the nursing home, we had a family graduation party for Kristine, and she opened her gifts. In all, it was a wonderful day.

The remainder of the month passed quickly. It was now June, and Brian and I were on the road to Houston to see Dr. White for Brian's check-up. He was feeling badly, so Dr. White put a STAT on his blood work. Brian was in a TTP episode…his platelets were down to 27,000. Dr. White admitted him to St. Luke's, and I drove him over to the hospital. They inserted a femoral catheter and began his plasmapheresis that afternoon…we were off and running. He was critical and in a semi-private room, so once again, I took up residence in the family room. His roommate was bedfast, so I was able to slip in about five each morning and take a shower while they slept.

For the first three weeks Brian was in the hospital, I didn't leave the hospital. He remained critical. I was afraid something would happen to him while I was gone. I kept clothes at the house in Conroe for emergencies, so Wallace brought them to me. I went to a washateria on Thursdays' …life was moving on. I called every other day to check on Marcy. She fully understood I couldn't leave Brian. He took his apheresis treatments daily, and the remainder of the I took complete care of him because with a femoral catheter and with his platelets so low, there is always the possibility of hemorrhage, thus he was not allowed out of bed. He was not responding to the treatments. His platelets were just sitting there...they weren't dropping but they weren't climbing either. Brian was already tired of the hospital... discouraged would be a better word. We had hoped that he was through with his TTP, hoping that God had seen fit to heal him...however, now we would once again have to run the race with patience.

Trials are inevitable in a Christian's life. They teach us endurance and suffering brings about true character as we keep our focus centered on God. It begins to conform us to be like Jesus. This is part of God's design for us, and we must bear in mind that the ultimate outcome of trials and suffering is designed for blessing if we *hang in, and keep the faith,* never giving up.

Not being able to go to Marcy was heart rendering. As I sat one morning thinking of all that was going on in our lives, it was almost too much. I felt as though I was being torn apart. Tears stung my eyes—I refused to shed them. It became important for me to behave as if life and the passing days were normal ones. I constantly put our problems in God's hands, and then I would take them right back knowing that He was in control. At the moment...l felt down right angry. I was tired of being a caregiver. You've heard the expression *get a life*, well I was ready for one, one without sickness. There were no tears now... anger had dried all of them. I decided it was time to stop my pity party and get on with the day.

Brian's blood work came back from the lab, and his platelets were 31,000. He was finally responding to treatment. I bathed him and changed his bed, went after some fresh water and told him I wanted to go check on Marcy. At the most, I would be gone about four hours. He agreed it was time to go see about her, that I needed to do this. I left the hospital feeling more positive than I had in weeks.

Marcy's Story

Just before I reached the nursing home, I stopped and picked us up some cappuccino coffee for a party. When I walked into Marcy's room, she looked at me. She was fighting with all her heart and strength not to cry. I moistened my lips, and fought the tears that stung my eyes. I was waiting for her to speak, but the words did not come. Finally, as I bent over to hug and kiss her, she said, "Mother, this has been the longest month of my life. I know you couldn't leave Brian...it's been so hard. We simply don't get any care at all. Sometimes it's an hour before they answer my light... I'm so tired of all this...l wish God would let me come home."

About that time the cleaning lady came into the room. She was a young Hispanic. In the past months, we had become friends. At one point, I told her that I was a music teacher, and that on my off periods, twice a week several Hispanic students came to my room, and I would help them with their English. She did not speak any English, so we always spoke Spanish. From time to time, I would tell Marcy what we were saying. She explained that when she had gotten to work that morning, she had stopped in to see Marcy, and that Marcy had gotten tired of waiting for them to answer her light had attempted to pull herself over on to her side to ease the pain in her back. She had gotten her head wedged in the corner of the bed and couldn't move. The maid went to the nurse's station and explained Marcy had needed help for an hour and could someone come. They said it would be a while... everyone was busy giving baths, and besides Hospice would be there soon and they could take care of it. She said she was not allowed to touch the patients, only clean their rooms. She said, "I closed the door, closed her curtain, and I pulled her down in the bed and freed her head. I didn't care if I lost my job...I thought what if this were my daughter lying here needing help so I moved her." I reached over and put my arms around her and hugged her and I began to cry. She cried, Marcy cried, we all cried, and I thanked God she had been willing to take the risk of helping Marcy and doing what needed to be done God had sent a helper. She said Marcy had explained that her Papa was malo, so she knew I couldn't come. I explained what was going on in Houston, and that my husband was very sick, and that this was the first time that I had been able to leave him. She said she would stop in to see Marcy as often as she could.

After she left the room, Marcy sighed and said, "Mother, would you please file for me a divorce? Gene walks in for ten minutes a couple of times a week...it upsets me that he doesn't stay... I'd rather he didn't come if he is going to rush in and rush out so he can get to the bowling alley. Will you do this for me?"

"Honey, we discussed this before. You have to have insurance, so you have to stay married. When Hospice moved you out of the mobile home, you became separated...this will have to do. Just try not to let him upset you...it doesn't do any good. Until Brian is out of danger, I have to stay at the hospital. Once they pull the femoral catheter and put one in his subclavian artery, he will be able to get out of bed...then I can leave him more. I have to drive to Lakeway this weekend to check on things. I haven't been home for over a month. I need to mow the lawn if I can get someone to teach me how to drive the tractor mower. Our neighbor is collecting our mail. I have to go to the Post office and make arrangements to have them hold it during the week, and deliver it on Saturdays. Things are really in a mess... but now that Brian's platelets are beginning to respond I'll be able to come up here more. I'll get it all worked out... you'll see."

"I brought us some cappuccino coffee...let's party!" We sat and visited while we waited for Hospice to come. The hour flew past and I needed to get back to Brian. Hospice still hadn't come so I bathed her from the waist down and changed her diaper. I wanted to know she was comfortable while she waited for them. I talked to the medications nurse. I asked her if Gene was coming to visit Marcy much. She replied, "Well I don't think you can really call it a visit, he's in and out in about five minutes."

Marcy's Story

Sighing I responded, "I thought perhaps she was losing track of time. Her mind seems fine...but we won't know what kind of memory loss she's going to experience with her brain tumor until it happens. I don't know why he bothers if that's all he stays... doesn't make sense to me. I have to get back to Houston. I told Brian I would only be gone about four hours total, so I have to get on the road. He's bedfast until they change his catheter over to his subclavian artery. He's not comfortable with women caring for him, so I do it all. Please look in on her when you can...the days and nights are very long when you are trapped in bed. Thanks for all you do. I'll see you when I can."

I walked back to Marcy's room. Brenda, her hospice person was there. I told her I had bathed her from the waist down and she said she would do the rest.

I walked to Marcy's bed. "Honey, I have to get back to Houston. Unless something happens, I'll be here next Tuesday. I walked over and put a big X on her calendar on Tuesday. Now that Brian is better, I can come more often." Tears of pain stung the back of my eyes. "I love you so much! Keep the faith, Honey... we'll get through this."

She made a feeble attempt to smile. I could see tears gathering in her eyes. "Don't worry about me, Mother. You just take good care of Brian...he's been so good about sharing you with me...I couldn't have made it this far without you and my Heavenly Father...we'll all just have to keep on keeping on. I love you...I'll see you on Tuesday. Give Brian a big hug for me... tell him I'm praying for him. Until then."

I took her into my arms and prayed, *"Father, I thank you that You have promised in Your Word that You will never leave us. I ask You to watch over Marcy, comfort her, let her feel Your presence. Bless all her caregivers. Please free her of the pain and loneliness as only You can. Thank you for all You are doing in both hers' and Brian's lives, we love You and praise Your name, in Jesus' name I pray. Amen!"*

I kissed her and hurried from the room before she saw me cry.

When I reached the car, I dissolved into tears. The agony of the moment was overwhelming. To leave her felt as though it was tearing out my heart...as I cried, I tried to still my thundering heart. She was totally helpless, apart from feeding herself. I breathed a prayer.

"Heavenly Father, I give You this mess...I can't handle all this. Please give me strength to care for them...to be Your person as I walk before others, reflecting that in You all is well, please help me Father, in Jesus' name I pray, Amen!"

I dried my eyes, took a deep breath and started the engine. I was on the road to Houston...to Brian.

When I walked into his room, he was asleep. I was glad of the opportunity to sit and rest and do some thinking.

My thoughts turned to Marcy. Marcy was unique. God simply didn't make them any better. She was beautiful in her faith. Her goodness, her kindness and selflessness constantly showed through her grief and pain. She worried about the effect her illness was having on us as a family. We in turn attempted to reassure her that her welfare was our major concern.

Brian turned over and opened his eyes. "You're back. How was Marcy?"

"She was really in a mess when I got there. She was having a lot of pain and they wouldn't answer her light, so she attempted to turn herself over. She was too far up in the bed so her head got wedged. The cleaning lady came in, saw what had happened and went for help, and she was informed Hospice would be there soon, and they would straighten her out. She said even though she wasn't allowed to touch the patients, she shut the door and pulled her down in bed. She said I thought about what if this was my daughter, and I did what was necessary. I hugged and thanked her for us. I explained how sick you were...that I was having to stay with you until you were able to get out of bed. She promised to look in on Marcy when she could. She's a good Catholic, and a good sister in Christ. Marcy sent you a big hug and she said she was praying for you. That's about all she can do now, lay there and pray for others. She wanted a divorce... said Gene came and stayed just long enough to upset her...five minutes or so. I talked with the nurse, and she said that was how it was working. I thought Marcy might be loosing track of time, but she's not."

"Hon, I've got some good news. They are going to change my catheter to my subclavian tomorrow. Once I can get out of bed, and have bathroom privileges, this will free you so you can be with Marcy more. See, just when we thought things couldn't get worse, they are suddenly a little better. I bent over, and hugged him...that's from Marcy, and I hugged and kissed him...that's from me."

The day passed and it was finally bedtime. After I got Brian ready for bed, I went out to the family room and made my chair bed...I longed for the day when I could sleep on a bed again. I was totally exhausted. One moment, I was freezing, and the next moment I was burning. My body was as confused as I was. The agony of the moment, of Brian and Marcy, had descended upon me, they were both so sick and needy, and then mercifully as sleep came, I didn't feel anything at all.

Everything went well with Brian's catheter. His platelets were still slowly creeping upwards and he was no longer confined to bed. Dr. White gave his approval for me to leave so all was well. Brian wanted me to go to Lakeway to pick up our mail and do the yard. Wallace had driven over and mowed it once so it was long past time for it to be done again.

I was on my way home. I was going to be gone from the hospital for two whole days. I was filled with excitement...I was going to be sleeping in a bed for the first time in nearly five weeks. Three and one-half hours later, I drove into the driveway. The yard definitely needed to be mowed... but everything appeared fine. After I opened up the house and unloaded my car, I called the church to let them know I was home. Pastor Gene answered. Everyone was delighted that Brian and Marcy were well enough for me to leave. After catching up on the church news, I took a long shower, microwaved me a frozen dinner and tackled the mountain of mail that Richard had brought over.

I didn't last long... too tired, and the bed looked too inviting. I decided I would stretch out and rest awhile... foolish me, the next thing I knew, it was morning. It was a beautiful day, warm and sunny.

After breakfast, I was sitting in my recliner enjoying my coffee reading the book on the mower trying to figure out how to start it when the doorbell rang. When I answered the door, there stood Howard and Helen Johnson, Howard was our Sunday school teacher, and Pastor Gene. We had a wonderful visit, and a sweet prayer time for Brian and Marcy. As they were leaving, Howard commented on the yard needing to be mowed. I explained that was one of the reasons I had come home...I just needed someone to teach me how to run the tractor mower. We walked to the garage and Howard showed me how to start the mower. He drove it out and mowed one side of the front yard. He offered to do the whole yard, but I insisted he had done enough.

After they left, I mowed the rest of the yard. It took some doing mowing around the rock walls and around the flower beds. The mower drove like a car except the brake was where the accelerator should have been, and the gas feed was on the

Marcy's Story

fender. I also had trouble guiding it. My neighbor came over and used his weed eater along the back wall... so we looked good.

I went in took a shower and then decided to clean the house. I enjoyed every minute of it...I was so thankful to be home. During the remainder of the day, practically everyone in our church family from Marshall Ford Baptist Church called to welcome me home. I called and checked on Marcy and Brian... they were both doing well. After lunch, I began working on the mail. I finally succeeded and when I finished, I was surprised to discover it was nighttime. The day had flown past. I decided to read awhile in bed and I discovered I was too tired to hold the book. I turned off the light and night slowly descended eclipsing the room and before I knew it, I was lost in sleep.

Sunday morning dawned and I quoted my thank you scripture.

"It is a good thing to sing praises and give thanks to the Lord, O most High, to declare his loving kindness by day and His faithfulness by night."

I went to the kitchen, made coffee and fixed me a waffle. While I was finishing my coffee, I read my Sunday school lesson. Afterwards, I dressed and drove to church where I received lots of hugs. It was so good to be in the Lord's house and be with my Christian friends. Martha the church pianist called in sick, so I played the piano for our church service. After church, some of us went out to dinner. After we ate, I changed into my shorts in the restroom, and once again, I was on the road to Houston.

When I arrived at the hospital, wonder of wonders, I found a place to park. I hurried up to Brian's room. He had just gotten a new roommate. This meant I would be sleeping in the family room as usual. The only time I could stay in the room with Brian at night was when he didn't have a roommate. He was from Vietnam, and he spoke some English. When I was telling Brian about playing for church that morning, he spoke up that he was a

Christian and also Baptist. Later that evening, his pastor came to visit him. When he was leaving, Sam explained we were Baptist too, and his pastor said he would like to pray for all of us. He didn't speak English, so Sam had been interpreting for him as we talked. We joined hands and bowed our heads and he prayed. Brian and I didn't understand a word he said, but we all felt the comforting presence of the Holy Spirit. We knew without a doubt in our hearts and minds that that the Holy Spirit was hearing and honoring the prayer.

For a few minutes we continued to hold hands as tears came into our eyes; we were reminded that when we have accepted Christ, and asked Jesus into our hearts and lives, to be our Savior, we are truly all brothers and sisters in Christ, no matter the race or color. We hugged each other, none of us breaking the silence, and he left. It was truly a special moment in time.

The weeks passed slowly. I usually drove to see Marcy on Tuesdays and Thursdays, and drove to Lakeway on Friday to do the lawn and mail. Brian didn't want me to hire it done. He didn't want anyone to know we weren't living in the house. Sometimes at church on Sunday when Bernadine had to be gone, I played the organ or piano or sang in the choir. Occasionally I sang a solo or Martha Woods, my close friend and I sang a duet, sometimes we sang with Jim in a trio...whatever needed to be done, I was happy to have a place to serve. This helped me keep anchored. I continued to drive back to Houston after we ate on Sunday afternoon.

For the next three months, this was our life. On the fourth month, I took a furnished apartment near the Medical Center. After attempting to sleep and live in the waiting room all these months, it was wonderful. Brian was finally well enough to be released from the hospital and he moved to the apartment. We did his plasmapheresis treatments as an outpatient. It became more difficult for me to spend time with Marcy. When Brian moved to the apartment, I was his twenty-four hours a day caregiver. Marcy understood, but it was so difficult, her being alone so much of the time. Gene was in and out, and Kristine usually visited when she knew I was coming. Hospice continued to bathe her and did her pain management, but even so, her back pain was still excruciating. The pain medicine made her nauseated, and it was difficult for her to keep her food down. It tore my heart knowing she was so alone and helpless facing the days with only God as her helper.

On December 24, six months from the time that Brian had begun his TTP episode, he was released. No more plasmapheresis...his platelets were back to normal. I loaded the blazer and we moved back to Lakeway. I felt like shouting for joy the whole time I was driving us home. Wallace and his friend, Mona, arrived and hour later, and Wallace helped me get Brian settled in.

Christmas day was wonderful...home at last. We truly celebrated our wonderful Lord's birthday with joy. Wallace caught up on the yard work for me before he returned to Conroe, so life indeed was looking much better. If only there weren't the anguish concerning Marcy. I continually lifted her needs to the Lord in prayer. Wednesday came and Brian suggested I go to Conroe and check on her. He felt he was strong enough to manage one day without me. I grabbed a change of clothes and jumped in the car and I was on my way.

I reached the nursing home about three that afternoon. Marcy's light was on. She had become nauseated and lost her lunch on the front of her gown and no one would come and change her. In desperation, she had covered her chest with a towel because the odor was making her more sick. I went to the office and asked the CEO to come with me.

As we entered the room, the smell from her nausea spoke louder than any words I could have spoken. I explained that she had been waiting for two hours with her light on for someone to come and help. He said he would take care of the matter. I attempted to talk with him, but my eyes swam with tears, and the more I attempted to gain control over my feelings of anguish and desolation, the more I cried.

Finally I was able to ask, "What would you do if this were your daughter?" He patted my shoulder and said, "I will take care of this."

As he left the room, I bent over and hugged her. She put her arms around me and said, "Mother, don't cry." And then, we both cried. After a few minutes when our tears were under control, I went to the supply cart for towels and washcloths to bathe her. As I was changing her into a clean gown, the nursing assistant came. She apologized for it taking so long for Marcy's light to be answered. I was feeling frustrated and angry...the worst part, I knew in my heart I was powerless to change what was happening to Marcy. Finally, fighting for control, I replied.

"I hope you never have to experience the anguish of your child having cancer...being totally helpless and dependent on others for her every need."

I turned away, forcing myself not to say more...forcing myself to be God's person instead of an angry hurt crushed mother. I turned and walked to the window and looked out at the parking lot until she left.
After a time, Marcy said, "Mother come talk to me. I don't want to waste a minute of your visit. I'm really O.K. Tell me about Brian."

This was the usual Marcy...always concerned about others. I explained he was doing pretty well...just weak. The bottom line was the doctors didn't know what to expect. His kidneys were beginning to fail... and if this continued, he would have to be on dialysis before too long.

Marcy's Story

"Mother, tell him I pray for him all the time."

"I know honey, we pray for you all the time. Our family has had its share of sickness. You know God is not the author of sickness and disease, but He does use them to mold and conform us into the person He desires for us to become. I take comfort from reading God's word. I know it's difficult for you to hold your Bible with one hand, but keep trying."

Sighing she replied, "Mother my eyesight is going. When I attempt to read, everything is blurred. My glasses don't help at all. I can still watch TV and read the close caption, but I can't read small print anymore. An optometrist was here last week and I signed myself up, and they took me. He checked my eyes carefully and said there was nothing he could do. My brain tumor is taking its toll."

For a moment, I could not think of any comforting words. "Honey, you know Dr. Goldenberg told us to expect this...I know you are weary of attempting to accept and rise above all that keeps happening to you, but all of this is part of God's plan for you, so you have to hang in! Sometimes words sound so empty, but we have to wait in faith for God's solution. You can continue to watch Channel 21, the religious TV station, and study God's word this way. Regardless of what's going on in our lives, I know we must trust God to the end, and as Churchill once said, "Never, never, never give up."

The remainder of the day passed quickly. I stayed and got her ready for bed and then drove to Conroe. I took a shower, called Brian and went to bed. I was totally physically and emotionally drained.

The next morning, I arrived just as Marcy was waking up. I sponged her off, and went to the dining room for coffee for us. We talked until her breakfast came and I helped her eat and brush her teeth. A little later, Hospice came and did their morning routine. I sat and visited with them while they bathed her and changed her bed. Marcy was quieter than usual. I knew she was thinking that after lunch I would be leaving and once again, she would be alone. The morning passed. I helped her eat lunch, and after lunch, I got her ready for her afternoon nap.

"Honey, you know I have to get on the road. I promised Brian I would be home before five. He's really weak, but he insisted I come. I know the new year coming doesn't look too inviting, but thank goodness God can take the mess our lives are in and use it for His glory...and as you know, that's why we are here, to glorify Him. I know that you are thinking at this point you wonder if you have the strength to go on. Once again, you will have to rely on your favorite scripture, *"I can do all things in Christ, who strengthens me,"* until God sees fit to change both our circumstances. I'll come one day next week, I can't say when... Brian has to see the doctor in Austin who will be caring for him in between our visits to Dr. White. Start every morning with your quiet time as you've always done, ask God to be your Comforter during the day and He will. He can be with you like no other... remember, God moment by moment is with you in this. I bent over and kissed her goodbye. "Next week, Honey, until then, God keep you."

She smiled as tears began to form in her eyes and signed, *I love you* in sign language. I signed *I love you* back to her, and left the room. In the car, once again, I gave way to my tears. I knew I needed to start home, and after a time, I finally was able to gain control over my emotions and leave.

Reaching the Goal

CHAPTER EIGHTEEN

The new year was ushered in. It was our prayer that our circumstances would change for the better. Once again, we established a new routine. I usually drove to Conroe to see Marcy one day a week returning the next day after lunch, depending on when I could leave Brian. He was not doing well at all...he was very weak. His platelets were drifting slowly downward. The months were passing slowly. Some months his platelets were up a little higher but mostly they continued spiraling downward.

I continued to drive to Conroe to be with Marcy. Things were pretty much the same...no improvement and still not much care.

One morning when I arrived, Hospice had phoned and said they could not come that morning. It was whirlpool bath day for Marcy's side of the hall, and they had taken her for one. She was delighted. When they brought her to her room, they had helped her into her chair and not using the lift, they had forgotten to put the lift portion under her. When it came time for her to be put back to bed, the two aides decided to lift her. Marcy and I were sitting there enjoying our visit. When they explained, they were going to lift her back to bed, I said, "Please get the lift. She's like a bowl of jello...hard to hang on to." They explained they lifted people all the time that were much larger than she was and not to worry.

I answered, "Please use the lift. She's so difficult to handle."

They patiently said I was not to worry...this was commonplace for them.

Marcy's Story

I stood up and walked over to Marcy. "At least let me help...I will lift her legs."

They shook their heads no, moved her chair facing the bed, raised it, counted and lifted. As they began to turn her, her legs gave way and she toppled. The three of them fell across the bed on their backs, Marcy hitting her back on one side of the bed, and her head on the other. I quickly reached down picked up her legs, and we spun her around into the bed.

"Mother, I think I've hurt my back again. The pain is really bad... will you ask them to bring me something for pain?"

I hurried to the nurses' station and explained what had happened. The nurse called for the radiologist to come with the portable x-ray machine and take some x-rays. After they were developed, they explained the doctor would be coming to talk to us. In the meantime, they decided to take her to the orthopedic surgeon by ambulance. I knew they had not liked what they had seen. After the new x-rays were taken, we waited for the doctor.

I wanted to scream with the waiting, with the anguish, with the denial that once again she would have even more pain to endure. As we waited, I kept thinking, *Heavenly Father what's going on? How much Lord, how much...I don't understand... surely not another fracture! Please God—no more—no more!*

A short time later, the doctor entered the room and explained that she had fractured another vertebra in her spine. There wasn't anything that could be done, just manage the pain and keep her in bed.

I knew her bones were fragile from all the chemotherapy, but this was ridiculous...another fracture. As we returned to the nursing home, I glanced over at her...I had difficulty focusing because of the tears that swam in my eyes. Her head was bowed

Marcy's Story

from the anguish and the pain she was feeling. What could I say? I was totally at a loss for words... no words of comfort...in fact, as I thought about it, I was downright furious. This need not have happened if only they had listened.

Finally, she lifted her head and attempted a smile through the pain.

"Mother, you've heard the saying, just when I thought things couldn't be worse...they got worse, Mother, I don't want you to be upset with what I am going to say...I ready for my new body...I have flat out worn out and ruined this one...I'm ready *"to be absent from this body and in the presence of the Lord...* "I really mean it, Mother". She smiled and we laughed at what she had said, then we cried. The paramedic who was in the ambulance with us turned his head, but not before I saw the sheen of tears in his eyes.

Finally, when I felt I could talk, I leaned over and took her hand. "Honey, I memorized two new scriptures this week...they are wonderful, and they fit the time."

1) "Praise be to the God and Father of our Lord Jesus Christ, the Father of compassion the God of all comfort.

2) Who comforts us in all our troubles, so that we can comfort those in any trouble with the comfort we ourselves have received from God. "

2 Corinthians: 3:4

"I know another fracture doesn't make much sense at this point in time but once again, you will have to rise above the pain and suffering as the scripture states, and to the best of your ability, in your affliction and in your suffering, in the deep trouble that you are in, I think God would have you act as an encourager to comfort others, to all who enter your room...to comfort them as He's going to comfort you, I guess as the scripture states, that's your responsibility in this matter. We will have to make a commitment to stop worrying about things that are beyond our control and place our faith and hope in God's ability to change you and your circumstances in His timing. There is hope because Christ is interceding for you in every area of your life. I know you are tired of trying to be strong but you can't stop fighting until it's His time."

We arrived at the nursing home and she was carefully put to bed and heavily sedated. I sat beside her bedside as she slept. Nahum 1:7 flashed through my mind. *"The Lord is good, a refuge in times of trouble. He knows those who trust in him."* We would simply have to keep trusting.

They brought in her evening tray. I awakened her and told her I would feed her.

She shook her head, "Mother, you eat it, I don't feel like eating anything. Would you get me cleaned up for bedtime and just let me rest?"

"Of course, Honey. I'm not hungry either...we'll just send it back."

I sponged her off and by the time I finished, she was ready for more pain medicine. I walked to the nurse's station, and a short time later they brought it to her. Afterwards, I kissed her goodnight, and waited until she fell asleep and drove to Conroe. My heart was heavy. I felt I was ready to shatter into a million pieces. I could not make sense of all that was going on in her life... one calamity after another. For that matter, Brian was growing worse daily. I wondered where all this was going to end.

Wallace was driving into the driveway as I arrived. I parked and got out of my car and walked over to him.

"How is she, Mother?"

I looked up to answer and the dam broke. I burst into tears. He walked me into the house. I brokenly explained to he and Mother that they had fractured her spine. They sat quietly, and let me cry it out.
Wallace asked, "What are you going to do about it?"

"Probably nothing, " I replied. "I'm sure she's going to say since God allowed it to happen, she will simply live with it. You know she's not one to make waves. I think at this point, she wants what measure of peace God allows. She told me she was ready to be in the presence of the Lord...her body was worn out. I'll know more when I see her in the morning...she's heavily sedated for the pain. I'm going to call Brian and check on him, take a shower and go to bed. This day has been incredible. I love you both, goodnight!"

After my shower, in bed, I attempted to pray. I was so distressed, my mind simply refused to function. Finally, the darkness closed in on me and I was grateful for the oblivion of sleep.
The next morning, she was still in a great deal of pain. I knew I had to ask what she wanted me to do. "Honey, you know this fracture was a nursing home booboo. I specifically asked them to use the lift and they made a very big mistake. Would you like for me to see an attorney?"

"No, Mother. The damage is done. It would just cost them their jobs. That won't help my situation ...it would be difficult for them to find another job...since my life is pretty well over, we'll just leave it alone. OK?"

"Whatever you want," I replied sighing.

Marcy's Story

Brenda, from Hospice came and bathed her and Linda checked her over. She said she would increase her pain medicine even more in attempt to keep Marcy comfortable. Her left leg was swelling and turning black indicating it had been injured in the fall. They placed her on an antibiotic and elevated it. A short time later they left.

I sat quietly by her bed. She lay there with her head turned toward me watching me. We were both thinking that I would soon be leaving. I was trying to still my aching heart.

"Honey, I have to leave. Brian is really sick. I asked him if he would let me pick him up and come stay in Conroe for a few days until you were better. He said he felt too badly to make the trip. I have to go to Lakeway. We'll just have to depend on Lynn and Hospice. I'll call Kristine and she can come and stay some after school…can't stand the thought of leaving you, but I must."

I stood and took her hands. *"Heavenly Father, we can't begin to understand why this happened. She's been through so much. We know it's not always Your plan for our loved ones to be healed, and we accept this…we accept Your will. We praise You for Your continual presence in her life, in both our lives, in all our lives… we can't go through this without You. We give You, her pain. Please take it from her…I place her in Your hands…you know I have to go to Brian. Bless Brian and heal him. Help him to feel stronger and better so I can help Marcy more. Father, we await Your solution. We love You, in Jesus' name we pray, Amen."*

"Mother, would you join me in praying for God to let me come home…I'm so tired. I really meant it yesterday when I told you I wanted to be in His presence."

"Of course, I will Honey. Try to sleep awhile. I'll be calling to check on you. God Bless!"

Marcy's Story

We signed our *I love you* and I left.

In the following weeks, I drove to Conroe whenever Brian was strong enough for me to leave him. It was time for his checkup. They called that afternoon when his lab results came in, and he was in another TTP episode. The doctor wanted me to bring him to Austin Diagnostic immediately to be hospitalized so they could begin his apheresis treatments. He informed them he did not want to be hospitalized and that since his catheter was still in place, he would take his treatments as an outpatient. His TTP was now chronic. He could have episodes at anytime.

I drove him to the hospital, and three hours later after his treatment was complete, we were on our way home...in all, it took five hours. I called Marilyn and told her she would have to go explain to Marcy that I could not come until Brian's platelets were built up enough... until he was out of danger...that he had refused to go to the hospital, and I couldn't leave him.

A month passed before I could leave Brian. One morning when Brian awakened, he said he was feeling stronger and he insisted he could drive himself to the hospital. He wanted me to follow him there to make sure he made it and then he wanted me to go on to see about Marcy. I made him promise to call the church if he was too weak to drive home. I knew Pastor Gene would be glad to pick him up. He drove fine. I helped him inside. The nurse said she would pick up his car from the parking lot and bring it to the door. He promised if he felt too weak to get from the car into the house, he would drive to our friend Martha's house and get her to help him inside. Everything was arranged...I was on my way at last.

When I arrived at the nursing home, as I approached Marcy's door, I heard her laugh and say, "I know Sam... you are the in-charge person here... do it."

Marcy's Story

I entered the room surprised to find Marcy alone in the room. I bent over and kissed her hello. "Honey, I thought I heard you talking to someone as I was coming down the hall. "Whom were you talking to?"

She smiled and answered. "I was talking to my new friend Sam. His voice comes through the speaker. We talk a lot...he works up front somewhere...he's good company. Sam, this is my mother. Her name's Tommye. Mother, say hello to Sam."

"Hi, Sam. Marcy honey, you can't hear when someone speaks on the speaker. You read lips—remember?"

Patiently she replied, "Mother, I can hear Sam. Didn't you hear him say hello when I introduced you?"

"No Honey, I didn't hear anything."

"Don't worry Mother, I'll tell you what he's saying. How is Brian? How could you get away?"

"He's a little better. He drove himself to the hospital. I followed and helped him inside. If he doesn't feel like driving home after his treatment, he's to call Pastor Gene. Martha's on standby if he needs help getting into the house. We were anxious to see how you were."

"Mother, I'm fine. Since Sam has been checking on me and talking to me, I'm not so lonely. Things are much better. He's constant company. I don't know when he ever goes home... he seems to always be around night or day whenever I need him. "

"Marcy, that's wonderful! I'm so glad you have a new friend. Have you met him in person yet?"

"No, Mother, he can't leave the front. He told me to talk to him

Marcy's Story

when I was lonely, so I do. That's all I can tell you."

"Honey, I'm going to talk to the med. nurse. I'll be back in a few minutes."

I walked down the hall to the medications cart. In a few minutes the nurse came out of the room.

"Hi! How have you been?"

She replied, "I've been fine. Busy-busy as usual. How is Mr. Hayden doing?"

"He's a little better. He drove himself to the hospital for his treatment this morning. I'm asking the good Lord to help him make it home safely. Listen, when I came down the hall this morning as I approached the room, I heard Marcy talking to her new friend, Sam. Has she mentioned him to you?"

"Yes, she has. She told me she hears his voice through the speaker."

I responded. "You know that's impossible. She can't hear anything...she lips reads totally. Her mind seems fine. She's as lucid as she can be regarding everything else. What do you think is going on?"

"We really don't know what's happening. The doctor examined her and she's doing as well as can be expected."

"Did he think it was her brain tumor?"

"No, since her body is so far gone, he feels the next symptom we will see will be blindness, and she's fine in that respect. She's much happier now, so we are counting it good."

"I guess I had better get back down the hall. Thanks for

everything you do. I'll talk to you later."

When I reached the doorway, I heard her speaking again. "Would you please come down and meet Mother? She thinks I'm nuts, and the only way she will be convinced that you exist is if you come." She appeared to be listening..."You can't come? Well, if it turns out you can, come on. You know me... I'm always here right in this old bed. I'll talk to you later. Mother will be back any minute so I'll hush. I know she thinks I've lost it."

"Well Marcy, I checked up on you, and everything seems to be going along fine. It's almost lunchtime. Can I get you anything?"

"No, Mother, I'm fine...it's wonderful your being here. I have really missed you. Do you know how long you can stay?"

"I will call Brian after lunch. If he made it home O.K., I will go home tomorrow. If he had problems, I'll have to go home tonight."

"Mother, I've been thinking. I know I won't be here much longer. I would like to write some letters to Kristine for her to have after I'm gone. I thought one now, one for when she marries, one for when she has her first child and else, we have time for. Can we do one today?"

"Of course, Honey, I think that's a great idea. Do you have some paper?"

"There's some in the night stand over there."

I walked over and found the tablet and sat down beside her bed. "I'm ready!"

"Dear Kristine, Mother will write this for me. My hands don't work too well anymore. I wanted to say a few things to you.

Marcy's Story

I want you to know I loved you before you were born. You were so special and you were the best baby—always had a ready smile.

As you grew older, I loved you even more. You were always musically inclined...always singing. It's no surprise to me how well you did with your clarinet and band.

I rejoiced when you accepted Christ as your Savior. I knew we would share eternity together. When you marry and have children of your own, you will understand, and it will be 'a praise the Lord' time when they accept Christ.

If God sees fit for me to come to Him, please raise my grandchildren to know and love the Lord as you have always done. Honey, please stay in church.

Memaw and I are praying for your mate. We want God's choice for your husband. Don't be in a hurry to get married. He will provide your husband in His time.

You have been wonderful this summer. I could not have made it without your help. I'm so grateful God gave me you for a daughter.

We will close. I'm tired I love you. Be the best person you can before God.

Love, Mother"

As we were finishing, her lunch came. I helped her eat...she didn't feel like eating much. Afterwards, I sponged her off and got her ready for her nap. For a time, I looked out her window letting my troubled and restless mind wander. She slept a little while. While she slept, I prayed. All our lives seemed so out of I glanced over at the bed and found she was watching me.

Smiling, I asked, "Why didn't you say something?"

"Mother, I knew you were either resting or praying, and I didn't want to disturb you."

"You didn't sleep very long."

"When you're here Mother, time is precious."

The afternoon passed all too quickly. Brian had made it home safely, so I would go home in the morning. After I helped her eat her evening meal, we got her ready for bed.

"Marcy, I'm really tired. I'm going to Conroe. I will be here first thing in the morning. You get some rest. I'll see you then. I love you so much! God bless...until morning." There was a lump in my throat that threatened to choke me. I had to rush from the room. I kissed her and drove home.

I visited awhile with Mother and Wallace. I called Brian...he was fine.

I said I would be waiting for him when he came home tomorrow. I took a shower and went to bed. It had been a very long day.

The next morning was a beautiful day, warm and sunny. On the way to the nursing home, I filled up my car and bought our cappuccino coffee. Marcy was looking out the window watching for me when I arrived.

"Good morning, Mother! I see you've brought coffee... I'm ready." We drank our coffee. After we finished, we had our quiet time. The morning passed so quickly. The thought of having to leave her again was beginning to make an aching feeling in my chest.

Marcy's Story

"Mother, I don't want you to worry about me. I know it's almost impossible for you to leave Brian. Things are much better since I have Sam to keep me company. One of these days when he has time, he will come to my room and I will get to meet him...meanwhile, it makes my long days pass...I'm really much happier... I'm really O.K. Trust me, I am managing fine. Please stop worrying about me... just do what you have to do to keep Brian going. I know you need to get on the road, so go! Come when you can...God willing, I'll be here. I love you so much. Now, go, go, go!"

I kissed her, looked up at the speaker. "Sam, thanks for keeping her company...look after her for me please while I'm gone. I'll be back as soon as I can. God Bless! I found a great scripture last night during my quiet time.

"I will listen to what God the Lord will say; he promises peace to his people, his saints... ''

Psalm 84:8

"You qualify Honey, you are one of God's saints. God's peace be with you. I love you; I'll see you soon."

As I drove towards Austin, I pondered the Sam thing. Could Sam be an angel? I was anxious to discuss this with Brian...to see what he thought. Whatever was happening, it was a positive thing. Her frame of mind was much better and I was thankful for that. I put in a Gaither CD, and sang along as the miles few past. Where would my life be without music?

Brian drove in a short time after I arrived home. I hurried to the garage to help him into the house. The three steps into the house were beginning to be very difficult for him. By the time he reached his chair, he was exhausted. He rested a few minutes and wanted to take a shower. He sat on his shower chair, and I bathed him and dressed him in his pajamas. I made a fresh pot of coffee and at long last, we were going to talk.

I brought in our coffee and he asked, "What's going on with Marcy?"

"I don't know," I replied. "Her body is gone... she's totally helpless, yet she's happier than she's been in months. I didn't really get into this over the phone...she has a new friend. His name is Sam. She's never met him. She explained he talked to her night or day, whenever she was feeling lonely. His voice comes through the speaker over her bed. I explained to her she couldn't possibly be hearing someone speaking through the speaker because her hearing was totally gone. She laughed and said I don't know why I can hear him and not anybody else, and I'm not going to question it...I enjoy having him for my friend, and now that you can't come very often, I'm thankful for him...he's good company. She introduced me to him...she was really surprised that I couldn't hear him. She laughed and told me he said we could pass for sisters. She laughed and answered cancer will do that every time. Her mind, other than the Sam thing, seems fine. Her eyesight is about the same. I talked to her nurse, and I asked if she could be hallucinating and she said her mind seemed fine...they really didn't have any explanation for what was happening. Honey, what do you think is going on... you're our spiritual leader...give me a clue as to what you think is happening."

"I've been thinking about it ever since you mentioned it over the phone. I knew you would be asking that very question. I believe because she's so alone now and that I'm in another episode, I believe God has sent her a Comforter in the form of an angel who speaks to her through the speaker. We both know she can't hear anything so what other explanation could there be? If she's happy, that's all that is important...you know God promises us He will never leave us...He's simply keeping His promise. We must be thankful the Comforter is present in her life. Apparently, her task is not finished here on earth... we will have to continue to be supportive until it is."

Shaking my head, I answered. "That's the conclusion I reached on the way home. Are we going to share what's happening with our church family?"

"For the time being," he answered, "Let's not say anything. We will just praise the Lord for His infinite love and continual presence in our lives."

Picking up my cup I walked over to his chair. "Do you want some more coffee? I'm going to see what I can find to fix for dinner."

He held up his cup, "Please."

After we ate, I took a shower and got ready for bed. I sat down to watch TV and found that I couldn't keep my eyes open.

"Honey, I'm falling asleep. I need to go to bed. Can you make it to bed by yourself? If not, let me help you now. You can watch TV in bed...I'm so tired, I don't think anything could keep me awake. Okay?"

"Sure, let's go."

I think I was asleep by the time my head hit the pillow. The next morning, I drove Brian to the hospital...we were off and running.

Great Expectations

CHAPTER NINETEEN

Slowly the weeks passed. I drove to see Marcy whenever Brian was well enough for me to leave him. He appeared to be getting gradually worse. His kidneys were failing...he would be on dialysis soon.

Marcy was growing somewhat weaker each time I saw her. She still was lucid and she still continually visited with Sam. She told me that now since she was having trouble speaking, he read her thoughts...wasn't that amazing... so they could still talk. She longed to be in the presence of the Lord. She asked for us to keep asking for our wonderful Heavenly Father to let her come home.

Her back pain was still excruciating...she took pain medication regularly, and this in turn, made her nauseated. Hospice said this would be for the remainder of her life. Now that I could not come and spend Monday through Friday with her as I had always done, our Conroe church family was faithful in visiting her. Dr. Herrington, our associate pastor, also checked on her. Her speech had grown much worse. She could hardly talk now... it took several minutes for her to say what she was attempting to say. This frustrated her, but she would just smile and keep trying until we understood what she was saying.

It was time for me to start for Austin. I had been sitting by her bed holding her hand when her brother Wallace walked into the room. We were both surprised to see him. He took one look at her and turned and walked to the entertainment center. He pretended to be adjusting the TV, but I knew he was attempting to gain control over the tears I had seen in his eyes. After a few minutes he came and sat down. For the next thirty minutes he kept us laughing telling us all the crazy things that had been happening to him. Marcy was delighted. She didn't try to talk, just laughed and watched him closely so she wouldn't miss anything… A little later, he said he had to get back to work. He bent over and kissed her on the forehead and she signed *"I love you."*

He turned and looked at me with a questioning look. I spoke, "She signed "I love you." He turned and smiling he signed, *"I love you."* He walked quickly from the room…I knew he was fighting the tears that had formed in his eyes,

She asked me to stop them from forcing her to eat. She said she would eat when she felt like it… however the smell of food made her so nauseated she could only eat a small portion. She grasped my hand and carefully spoke.

"Mother, if God wills that I come to Him before you come again, hold me in your heart until we meet again in the presence of the Lord."

I wanted to speak, but words would not come. I bent over and kissed her goodbye. Finally, I managed to answer,

"My brave wonderful daughter, you have truly *"fought the good fight and kept the faith."* I love you …until we see each other again."

As I was leaving her room, her friend Lynn arrived. We talked a few minutes in the hallway. I thanked her for being so faithful in helping and visiting Marcy and she replied, "I never leave her room but what I am blessed for having come. It helps me being with her."

We hugged and I left.

As I drove to Austin, I knew that it would not be long now until God answered our prayer and let her come home. The thought that I was going to out-live my child was heart wrenching. I cried most of the way home. I couldn't seem to get a grip on my emotions. She was so dear and so precious. I knew that if I didn't stop crying, my eyes would swell shut, and then I wouldn't be able to drive. I was not having a pity party...I was crying because her life had been so difficult...so tragic...all the things that had happened in the past thirteen years...and yet, she had faced each obstacle as it arose heroically with bravery and complete trust in God.

Free at Last... The Journey

CHAPTER TWENTY

The following week I drove Brian to Houston for his checkup with Dr. White. Although Brian was receiving his plasmapheresis treatments in Austin, Dr. White was still Brian's primary physician. His appointment wasn't until eleven thirty, so we drove by to see Marcy. He stayed in the car while I ran inside to check on her.

As I entered the room, I felt instantly that her time was near. Hospice had called and informed me they were increasing her pain medication to keep her more comfortable. I wanted this for her...I never again wanted to see her with her body wracked with pain.

I talked with her and patted her. She opened her eyes and smiled and closed them and settled once again into a deep painless sleep. I kissed her and left.

As I reached the car, I dissolved into tears. After a few minutes I dried my eyes and turned to Brian.

"She's dying."

"Did she know you?"

"Yes, isn't it amazing? It wasn't supposed to happen this way... she was supposed to be in a coma for several weeks. God is good."

We drove to Dr. White's office. He gave Brian a thorough check up.

Marcy's Story

We knew what was happening to Brian so we were not surprised at the results. We talked for a short time and left. As we were leaving the parking lot, I asked Brian if it would be O.K. for me to run by to see Marcy one more time. He explained he was worn out and he wanted to go to Lakeway...he needed his bed. I could drive back to be her in the morning if I felt it was necessary. We arrived home around 5:30 P.M.

I bathed him and put him to bed. I felt so tired I could hardly move.

I made tuna sandwiches and took him a tray into the bedroom. A short time later, when I went in to get his tray, he was sound asleep.

I called the nursing home, and they told me she was as low as she could be and be alive. I called Gene, and wonder of wonders, he was home.

"Gene, did you go see Marcy this afternoon?"

He replied, "No, this wasn't my day to stop by."

"Gene, I feel very strongly that she's going to *be in the presence of the Lord tonight.* This morning we drove by on our way to Houston...she's really low. Would you please go stay with her tonight? I don't want her dying alone. Will you go do this?"

"Tommye," he answered, I will check on her on my way to work in the morning. I'm really tired."

"Please, Gene, go stay with her. I'll make arrangements for Brian, and I will be there first thing in the morning… please don't leave her alone tonight."

He sighed and answered, "O.K."

Marcy's Story

I called the nursing home and told them Gene was coming to stay the night with her, and that I would be there in the morning. I asked them to call me if he left so I could send her sister, Marilyn to sit with her. I knew in my heart that tonight was the night. I called Marilyn and explained what was happening. We cried together for a few minutes. Finally, I managed to tell her that they were going to call me if Gene left, and that I would call her if the need arose for her to go stay until I could get there. She wanted to go on, but I said that I thought Gene needed this time to say goodbye... just to wait for my call.

I went to bed. I was heartsick...my chest was heavy and once again, cold trembles began. I wanted so much to be with Marcy... but I couldn't be...I had to accept this, however, at the moment I was incapable of logical thoughts. I was totally exhausted but sleep did not come. I waited for the phone to ring, and at one-thirty in the morning, it rang.
As I reached to answer, my heart began thundering in my chest. I knew it was over...then as quickly as my heart had begun its suffocating dance, I felt a sudden peace, only the peace that God alone can give.

"Hello!"

"Tommye, she's gone. She died an easy death. She sat up and gasped...I reached over and took her in my arms, and it was over. Thank you so much for insisting that I go. I'm so glad that I was with her."

"I'm glad you were too. Do you want me to come in the morning?"

"No, you know we made our funeral arrangements before she became so sick. I'll call you after I talk to the funeral home."

"We'll be home about two tomorrow after Brian's treatment. Call me then."

Marcy's Story

As I hung up the phone, Brian asked, "It's over?"

"Yes, it's done. Gene will call after we get home from the hospital tomorrow. Do you think the social worker can arrange for you to do your treatment in Houston the day of the funeral?"

"I don't see why not…you can check on it tomorrow while I take my treatment. Honey, have you slept any?"

"No, I was waiting for the call."

"Please Honey, try to get some rest … she's at rest now."

"I know." I sat on the bed totally dry eyed...no tears...it felt strange... Marcy was gone.

"Honey, lie down…you have to get some sleep."
I rested but did not sleep. In the morning, I called the church from the hospital. I told Pastor Gene that Marcy had passed away. I insisted that he tell our friends not to come...it was such a hard drive for a thirty-minute funeral. The social worker called Houston, and they would do Brian's treatment... they would work him into their schedule.

The phone was ringing when we entered the house that afternoon. Gene was calling to say that she was going to be buried from Brookhaven Funeral home in Houston.

"Gene, you know she wanted to be buried in Conroe... you know she planned her own funeral."

"I know, but the Kings are always buried in Houston."

"Well, that's not what she wanted, but I guess it's your choice.

"

Marcy's Story

He answered, "That's what I want. Will you go to Brookhaven with Kristine and me to plan the funeral?"

"Of course...when is the funeral going to be? We have to make arrangements for Brian's apheresis treatments to be done in Houston?"

He replied, "Sometime Friday."

"We will leave for Conroe from the hospital tomorrow. We should be in Conroe around two. We can go to the funeral home then. Will that give them enough time for the arrangements?"

"Yes, they told me all that really remained to be done was to print the program and set the time for the funeral. You know what her wishes were so you will have to give them the information."

"Fine! I have the pallbearer list with everyone's phone numbers here, so I'll call all of them tonight. Just give me a time."

He replied, "Let's set the time for three-thirty... O.K.?"

"That's fine. Do you want me to call the ministers, or do you want to do it?"

"You handle it."

"Gene, she wanted Everett to bring the message, and Dr. Herrington to do the eulogy. I have a feeling our pastor from our church here will appear even though I've insisted no one come... it's so far. He insisted on knowing the time for the funeral. If Pastor Gene comes, he can do the prayers and whatever else he feels necessary. She *wanted Footprints in the Sand read,* and me to sing *He Touched Me*. She wanted the congregation to sing *Heaven Came Down* and *Glory Filled My Soul*... that's pretty well it. Does that sound O.K. to you?"

Marcy's Story

"Tommye, I'll leave that to you since you know what her wishes were."

"I left her obituary in the drawer in my bedroom. Wallace will take it to the paper. Also, the gown I bought to bury her in is there. The photograph she wanted on her casket is also there. She does not want her casket open... she did not want anyone to see her, only the immediate family. Gene that was the one thing she made me promise... the casket closed. Please don't change that. I will have Wallace leave everything on the kitchen table. You will need to take it to the funeral home. We'll see you tomorrow afternoon. "

That afternoon, I mechanically made the necessary arrangements. I felt at peace as I made the calls. Still no tears... just comfort in knowing she was with the Lord...that her sweet spirit was no longer trapped in her body... she was at peace at long last.

Brian and I made it an early night. We were both worn out. As I lay in bed pondering tomorrow, exhaustion finally claimed me. I drifted into a shallow state of restless sleep. Fragmented dreams, floated to the surface of my mind. As morning dawned, I awakened drenched and shivering. I was thankful the long night was over.

Brian's treatment went well. We arrived in Conroe a few minutes before two. Gene and Kristine were waiting for me. I ran to the bathroom and freshened up. We drove to the funeral home and completed the arrangements.

The remainder of the day passed. I felt as though I was trapped in a vacuum. I was glad when night approached...I was tired of going through the motions of living.

The next morning, Brian drove himself to Houston. He was afraid something would go wrong during his treatment, and if we were delayed, we would miss her funeral. Marcy's Sunday school class brought food that morning, and Betty brought food from ours. We didn't feel like eating so we decided to wait until after the funeral. Wallace, Mother and Tristin rode together, and I rode with Gene and Kristine.

Pastor Gene had come from Austin and was waiting when we arrived. I met with the three pastors and we arranged the order of service. I then met with the person in charge of the music and gave him the tapes for *Heaven Came Down and He Touched Me*. We did a sound level so all was in readiness. I spoke a few minutes with my good friends, Carolyn and Al, and then went down to the front.

As I sat waiting for the time for the funeral to begin, I bowed my head letting the soothing music lull my sore heart. At long last, I felt like crying. I bit my lips to stop the tears. I would honor her bravery by being brave and honoring her wishes. I looked at my watch. It was time. As I rose to walk forward to sing, *He Touched Me,* I thought, *I will do it for her...* I swallowed the rising lump in my throat.

I took the microphone and spoke. "Two different times Marcy asked me to sing for her funeral. I explained to her that I wasn't sure I could keep it together long enough to sing."

She replied, "Mother I want you to sing for me...if you have to stop and cry, I'm sure no one will get upset with you...I simply won't take no for an answer. Please, Mother?"

"So, Marcy, with God's help, for you, *He Touched Me.*" The music began and God honored prayer...I sang. The remainder of the funeral went beautifully. It was a glorious victory, just as she had wanted.
They opened her casket afterwards for the family to view her for the last time. Pastor Gene walked with me to the casket. My

tears spilled over at last. She looked so beautiful in the Lord.

After the graveside service, as we were walking to the car, Dan and Martha Jane came over. Dan said, "Tommye would you like to know the last words Marcy said to me when we went to see her last week?" I nodded my head yes.

"I asked if I could do anything for her and she shook her head yes. It took her a few minutes to say it...but she finally said, "Pray." "I thought you would want to know."

I thanked him and we all hugged each other goodbye and we left for Conroe. When we got to the house, no one wanted any food, so Gene and Kristine took some home with them, I left some for Mother and Wallace, and Brian and I took the remainder to Lakeway.

On the way home, Brian reached over and said, "This morning, when they were taking me off the machine, a floating nurse came into the cubicle, and she heard me say that I needed to hurry so I could get to my daughter's funeral. I mentioned she had chemotherapy one week a month at St. Luke's for more than five years...that they had stopped the chemo when she developed three brain tumors. She spoke up and asked, "Was your daughter by any chance Marcy King, and her mother, Tommye?"

I answered, "Yes, how did you know...it's been three years since they discontinued her chemo...how can you remember that far back...you must have treated hundreds and hundreds of patients since then?"

She smiled and answered, "There was only one Marcy King. Your daughter was a truly special and unique person... to know her was to want to live a better more productive life. Her life of faith...the life she lived was life-changing for many of us as we grew to know her during her many hospital stays. "

Marcy's Story

"Honey, I thought you would want to know. She will be remembered...she truly made her life count for the Lord... proclaiming Christ with the life she lived...not just words... and that's what it's about."

We drove the rest of the way home without speaking... each thinking our own thoughts. As a family, we had longed and prayed for her healing...that had been our prayers---a wish never destined to be granted. The long grueling days without end had passed.

I pictured her whole...healthy...free. Marcy, my sweet daughter, the sturdy, the wise, fast moving, fast talking, always smiling, with her infectious laughter...whole at last in the presence of the Lord.

"Precious in the sight of the Lord is the death of saints His saints."

Psalm 116:15 (NIV)

Dear Reader Friend:

I hope in reading this you have caught the importance of trusting God for your every need.

Please apply the scriptures used to your own life situation. I encourage you to seek God for answers to your challenges, and seek His peace and His presence as you journey through your trials of life.

He is ever faithful!

Marcy's Story

I was born on an oil lease near Wewoka, Oklahoma. Throughout our school life, out teachers instilled in each of us a strong desire to learn and reach our highest potential.

After completing High school in three years, at age sixteen, I entered nurses training at Hotel Dieu in El Paso, Texas. I left school, married and had three children. Fifteen years later, my marriage ended in divorce. I had just completed my freshman year of college.

I obtained my Bachelor of Arts degree from the University of Texas in El Paso, (U.T.E.P.) in 1965. It was difficult pursuing a degree while raising and supporting three children, but with God's help, we managed.

After graduation, we moved to Conroe, Texas, where I obtained a teaching position. I taught school, worked summer vacations for two doctors, and served as choir director at First Baptist Church. As a single parent, three jobs were a necessity for our welfare. In later years I served in other churches.

I completed my Master's Degree from Sam Houston State University in 1970.

I married Brian Hayden in 1979. He became terminally ill in 1985, and Marcy became ill in 1986. I was their caregiver for sixteen years and thirteen years respectively.

I have one other published book entitled HIS WONDERFUL PRESENCE.

www.ingramcontent.com/pod-product-compliance
Lightning Source LLC
Chambersburg PA
CBHW071437080526
44587CB00014B/1889